CW00558074

RE**THINKING**

STRATEGY

RE THINKING

STRATEGY

HOW TO ANTICIPATE THE FUTURE SLOW DOWN CHANGE AND IMPROVE DECISION MAKING

STEVE TIGHE

WILEY

First published in 2019 by John Wiley & Sons Australia, Ltd
42 McDougall St, Milton Qld 4064

Office also in Melbourne

Typeset in 11pt/15pt Palatino LT Std

© John Wiley & Sons Australia, Ltd 2019

The moral rights of the author have been asserted

NATIONAL
LIBRARY
OF AUSTRALIA

A catalogue record for this
book is available from the
National Library of Australia

All rights reserved. Except as permitted under the *Australian Copyright Act 1968* (for example, a fair dealing for the purposes of study, research, criticism or review), no part of this book may be reproduced, stored in a retrieval system, communicated or transmitted in any form or by any means without prior written permission. All inquiries should be made to the publisher at the address above.

Cover design by Wiley

Cover and internal image © Pro Symbols / Shutterstock

10 9 8 7 6 5 4 3 2 1

Disclaimer
The material in this publication is of the nature of general comment only, and does not represent professional advice. It is not intended to provide specific guidance for particular circumstances and it should not be relied on as the basis for any decision to take action or not take action on any matter which it covers. Readers should obtain professional advice where appropriate, before making any such decision. To the maximum extent permitted by law, the author and publisher disclaim all responsibility and liability to any person, arising directly or indirectly from any person taking or not taking action based on the information in this publication.

To Sharon, for believing in me,
and Miliani, for inspiring me

CONTENTS

ACKNOWLEDGEMENTS

This book shares my accumulated learning from the past decade and a half of studying and practising strategic foresight, both from within a large multinational company and from working with similar-sized organisations as an external consultant.

My exposure to futures studies began at the Australian Foresight Institute (AFI) at Swinburne University where I was lucky enough to come under the tutelage of Joseph Voros and Peter Hayward. Instantly I appreciated the space they created for thinking about the future and, in the process, opening up a whole new way of seeing the world. This was especially true of their focus on worldviews and values, the hidden drivers of social behaviour and an oft-overlooked component of strategy. I still regard the lifetime work of psychologist Clare Graves, summarised in *Spiral Dynamics*[1] by Don Beck and Chris Cowan, as offering one of the most powerful tools for understanding and anticipating social change.

It was at Swinburne that I met Marcus Barber, whose initial support with implementing organisational foresight assisted me greatly. In my early days as Foresight Manager at Foster's, whenever I found myself asking 'Where do I start?' I turned to Marcus. His practical advice provided a handy counterbalance to the abundance of theories and models that exist within the futures community.

Through the AFI I was introduced to the thinking of Sohail Inayatullah, whose book *Questioning the Future*[2] continues to provide such clarity around how to think about social change and the future. Through the writings of Sohail I learned to appreciate the value of understanding the patterns of history as a guide to the future. His thought-provoking work with Robert Burke enabled me to see the central role that strategic identity plays in allowing organisations to adapt to the future.

The work of another Australian futurist, Richard Bawden, with his emphasis on experiential learning and *learning from the future*[3], strongly influenced my thinking about the purpose of scenarios and the design of scenario workshops. He helped me move on from the certainty of the future, to appreciate its uncertainty, and to bring the future alive in the minds of scenario participants.

Several colleagues from my decade at Foster's deserve special thanks. Bettina Freshney began the journey with me at Swinburne in 2004. We weren't sure what we were searching for, but we knew there had to be a better way to think about strategy and innovation. Justin Casey, the pragmatic CEO-in-waiting, continually urged me to pursue the 'so what?' challenge when my focus was too skewed towards exploring 'what's next?' Allan Brassil, a mentor who became a friend, continues to provide invaluable advice today.

Kara Rodden, Andrew Fairlam and Mark Truelson, the innovation A-team at Foster's, quickly recognised the strategic link between foresight and innovation, and fully supported my early attempts at scenario planning. When others were struggling to see the corporate benefits of scenarios, or when self-doubt began to cast its mighty shadow, it was the wisdom and support of this trio that reassured me I was on the right track.

While foresight is critical, hindsight is a wonderful thing. And looking back, it's clear that I've been fortunate to meet so many gifted thinkers and practitioners over the years—people who have helped me to constantly review and develop my philosophies and processes on the future, strategy and innovation. So, to the managers, tutors, mentors, friends, colleagues, clients and participants who have helped to shape and shared my experiences along the way, your influence is reflected within these pages.

EMPOWERING YOUR ORGANISATION

Strategic agency is possible in a time of volatility and uncertainty

In December 2003 I pondered a question increasingly at the forefront of every business leader's mind: *How do you get ahead of trends?* I had been working in the Consumer Insights department at global brewer Foster's (Carlton & United Breweries) for just on 12 months, and from my close vantage point I could see the limitations of our heavy reliance on market trends to guide innovation and marketing. We were a myopic and reactionary company, obsessed with our competitors and often surprised by shifting industry dynamics. We needed to broaden our outlook and to develop our anticipatory capabilities.

From this simple question, my career took a dramatic detour as I commenced my journey into the field of futures studies. While researching the word *foresight*, I was fortunate enough to discover that Swinburne University in Melbourne had actually established the Australian Foresight Institute. This was a stroke of luck. One of the few places in the world to offer a Master of Strategic Foresight degree was literally just down the road.

Four months later I found myself sitting in class imagining naively that I was about to learn how to predict the future. While this hope was quickly dashed ('What do you mean the future's not predictable?'), I instantly recognised the organisational value of what I was learning. So much so that in May 2004 I wrote to the Managing Director at Foster's, making the case for a new internal position: that of 'Foresight Manager'. I didn't know exactly what the role looked like, but my instincts told me there was a need for such a function. He agreed—and I was it.

So in June 2004, three months after starting my master's degree, and having only just worked out where the best coffee was served on campus, I commenced my role as Foresight Manager at Foster's. Essentially, I was charged with responsibility for understanding how the behaviours of Australians might change over the next 10 years, what future social wants and needs might emerge from these changed behaviours, and what the implications and opportunities might be for Foster's as a beverage company.

As I sat at my desk on the first day in my new role I still clearly remember the feeling of being overwhelmed by the complexity of the task. Indeed, the one clear thought I had at the time was *Where do I start?* The future appeared to me a vast, uncertain and unknowable black hole, seemingly awash with infinite possibilities. What was important? What was insignificant? And how would I know the difference? These were the questions running through my mind as I sat paralysed at my desk surrounded by colleagues purposefully going about their roles.

The difference, of course, was that my workmates fulfilled roles where the patterns of expectation and performance were well established. I, on the other hand, had seemingly stepped into the unknown. Such a role had not previously existed at Foster's, and corporate foresight managers were hardly prominent, so useful reference points were somewhat limited. What I needed at the time, and what every organisation needs today, is a framework for anticipating and preparing for future change. Something to help make sense of the patterns in the chaos.

Rethinking Strategy is the book I needed to read on my first day as Foresight Manager at Foster's.

The fundamental challenge

This book is about organisational empowerment. It provides the strategic insights and tools to empower managers to determine the future they want for their business.

Rethinking Strategy is based on the premise that environmental sensitivity, strategic transformation and strategic distinctiveness are the fundamental challenges for organisational empowerment and business success in the twenty-first century:

- In an increasingly uncertain environment, organisations must develop the sensitivity to anticipate emerging market shifts and turn future ambiguity into ongoing strategic advantage.
- In a time of constant change, organisations must be able to transform what they do, how they do it, even who they are, to remain relevant and achieve their future goals.
- In a time of expanding competition, organisations must be able to generate a distinct strategic outlook that differentiates them from competitors and provides a sustainable advantage into the future.

More than ever, these are the strategic challenges that confront and overwhelm business leaders today.

What they don't know is how to meet these challenges.

This inability to foresee and to adapt to significant changes in their business environment, to develop distinct strategies for the future, is the cause of great frustration and anxiety for managers, their boards and investors. It traps them in a cycle of responsiveness to external changes; it constrains them to clinging to strategies that have passed their use-by date; it forces them to adopt a scatter-gun or me-too approach to innovation; and it ultimately leads to corporate failure.

But companies don't have to die; strategies do.

What this terminal pattern points to is the failure of strategy and innovation processes to keep pace with increasingly volatile market conditions and the modern demands of business. Knowing no different, managers reluctantly return to the inadequate data sources and ineffective strategy processes they know but no longer trust. The result is increasing vulnerability to strategic surprises and a growing sense of disempowerment when it comes to influencing the future they want.

With volatility and uncertainty as the business norm, managers are searching for a new approach to take their companies forward, a process specifically designed to seize opportunity from uncertainty, a process that can generate a new and distinct strategic outlook, a process that mobilises the creative and entrepreneurial capabilities that lie within every organisation.

Rethinking Strategy presents such an approach.

It aims to restore the loss of organisational agency by providing an innovative process for strategy development that is purpose-built for today's volatility and uncertainty. Such a process reframes strategy as a resource and positions strategic design as the organisation's principal creative and learning activity. In doing so, *Rethinking Strategy* presents a complete and practical approach to address the three essential questions at the core of successful strategy development:

- What's next?
- So what?
- Now what?

Central to this process is the art of developing scenarios and an appreciation for the anticipatory and transformational capacity that scenarios enable. Scenarios empower managers to generate original strategic perspectives; to *reperceive* the future environments in which they might have to compete, and to *reconceive* the organisation's role and functions within these futures.[1] In doing so, internally generated scenarios help to deliver that rarest of business assets, a unique strategic outlook that is fit for the future. Such an outlook is the source of organisational distinctiveness.

Overview

This book follows the pathway of my journey from Consumer Insights Manager at Foster's to the emerging fields of futures studies and strategic foresight, and ultimately to the domain of strategic design. It pulls together the academic and practical experience acquired over this period to present methods for anticipating future change and an end-to-end process for strategy development as a catalyst for strategic transformation and distinctiveness.

This process is outlined in a logical sequence that captures the three distinct phases of my journey: *Searching, Learning* and *Doing*.

PART I: SEARCHING

Chapter 1: The trouble with trends. Managers are uncomfortable and frustrated with their organisation's unhealthy and often ineffective reliance on obvious market trends and industry-centric data sources. While trends are useful, the trouble with trends is that they don't illuminate future market shifts and they don't provide a competitive advantage. As a result of this dependence, organisations have become disempowered at a time of increasing turbulence and continue to suffer from foreseeable strategic surprises that disrupt their business models.

This chapter makes the argument that a different approach to strategy and innovation is necessary to recalibrate the loss of organisational agency in today's turbulent business environment. Scenario planning sits at the core of this approach.

PART II: LEARNING

Part II details the theories and methods, acquired and developed over the past 15 years, that underpin my approach to designing strategy.

Chapter 2: The latent resource. Scenario planning has been applied in business since at least the late 1960s, yet for all their promise, and despite their suitability to volatility and uncertainty, scenarios have enjoyed a mixed history, with few celebrated successes, widespread misunderstanding and ultimately unfulfilled potential. Key reasons for the failure of scenarios to make a greater impact on business strategy are presented for resolution in this chapter.

Chapter 3: Where does the future fit? Scenarios continue to be neglected by corporations because of a general lack of understanding around where they fit with business strategy and innovation. This lack of understanding and subsequent lack of integration is a key driver of business failure—managers simply don't have the skills to anticipate emerging discontinuities.

Defining strategy as *a plan for action to achieve your goals in perceived future environments* illuminates the role of futures thinking and places scenarios at the centre of strategic design. Scenarios provide strategic reasoning, the focal point around which the organisation's strategic positioning and objectives interact and evolve. From this definition, a logical process to develop strategy emerges.

Chapter 4: Reframing strategy. In turbulent times, the purpose of strategy is to generate a new and distinct strategic outlook that is *fit* for the future. Successful strategic design therefore requires the imagination to foresee future change and the innovative skills to apply meaning for the organisation.

This entrepreneurial approach to strategy reframes strategic design as the organisation's principal creative and learning activity. And the emphasis on creativity, participation and learning repositions strategy as a *process-oriented* activity, as opposed to being *output-oriented*.

Chapter 5: Overcoming myopia. Managerial passion, industry expertise and omnipresent data combine to produce a myopic vortex at the top of the organisation that seeps down through the lower reaches. Close-knit industries are especially prone to myopia and therefore vulnerable to strategic surprise because all the member companies look to each other for standards of best practice. This is the danger of industry benchmarking.

This chapter places the organisation and its industry within the broader context of a changing society, recognising that successful strategic design requires managers to overcome industry myopia and adopt a broad contextual outlook.

Chapter 6: The shape of things to come. The evolution of social change tends to follow the shape of a bell curve, passing through four distinct stages: an embryonic phase, an emerging phase, an established phase and an eroding phase. Rarely easy to detect, the ability to anticipate and prepare for the emergence of strategically significant embryonic issues and opportunities *before* they develop is perhaps the greatest planning skill an organisation can have.

This chapter introduces original methods for identifying embryonic issues and opportunities, providing managers with the tools to anticipate different future operating environments before they emerge.

PART III: DOING

As the business environment evolves, organisations must be prepared to transform and transition to new strategies to maintain their strategic fit with the external environment. Proficiency at strategic design therefore becomes more important than developing a one-time 'best strategy'.[2]

Part III moves on from the theory of strategic design to its application, describing an end-to-end process for scenario-based strategy development and using successful case studies to illustrate business practicality.

Chapter 7: The strategic challenge. Scenario planning starts with a strategic challenge: any pressing issue management considers strategically significant. This chapter describes the types of strategic challenge typically faced by organisations for which the use of scenarios is advantageous: these are innovative, specific and exploratory. It also offers guidelines to assist those about to embark on the process by providing an indicative timeline for effective scenario planning and criteria for setting the horizon year.

Chapter 8: How do I know what I think until I see what I say? The orientation phase of strategic design places an emphasis on internal interviews to understand managerial perceptions of the past, present and future. This qualitative research provides the necessary foundation for strategy formulation, yet remains overlooked in most processes. Extensive personal experiences are included to show how strategic insights can be extracted from these interviews. The output of these interviews then provides a framework for subsequent environmental scanning.

Chapter 9: Conversations with Mr Silly. This chapter explains the role of environmental scanning in the strategic design process. The purpose of scanning is not to trawl mindlessly through endless data but rather to identify potential drivers of future change that hold significance for the organisation and to stimulate thinking about what could be in the future. To achieve these ends, the personal, historical and external aspects of effective scanning are extensively covered, with particular focus on the limitations of industry experts and the need to collate and cultivate a collection of perception pioneers—outsiders who see the world and the future differently.

Chapter 10: 'What's next?'—Anticipating the future. Scenarios are the most effective vehicle for business transformation because they unlock strategic creativity. This chapter comprehensively details the process of creating scenarios including choosing the significant drivers of change, fleshing out different scenario worlds and backcasting from the future to the present. The result is a different, future context from which decision makers can assess strategic implications and options for their organisation.

Chapter 11: 'So what?'—Positioning for the future. Inability to extract strategic value is perhaps the greatest managerial frustration with the scenario process. 'So what?' addresses this longstanding issue by demonstrating how optimal interpretation and subsequent strategic positioning relies on a broad sense of corporate identity (*who we are, why we do what we do*). A broad strategic identity enables management to assess future opportunities from the widest practical platform, providing the flexibility to adapt to evolving social conditions, while remaining true to organisational purpose and heritage.

Chapter 12: 'Now what?'—Transitioning to the future. Achieving impact with scenarios relies on integration with the organisation's planning and operations processes. This integration is achieved via a strategic plan, which gives operational meaning to any longer-term strategic framework. Such a plan provides a direct line of sight between the scenarios and the organisation's day-to-day operations and priorities.

Chapter 13: Making sense of the patterns in the chaos. Scenarios build a corporate intelligence for anticipating and interpreting future change. They equip managers with a future memory of signals to scan for and provide reference points for attaching meaning as these events occur. The strategic benefit is increased sensitivity and preparedness for future discontinuities before they occur. Ongoing and purposeful monitoring of the external environment then feeds into the next round of scenario development, providing the organisation with a dynamic, integrated and repeatable strategy process.

Further resources on scenarios, strategy and innovation can be found at www.stevetighe.com.au.

PART I
SEARCHING

CHAPTER 1

The trouble with trends

Information must illuminate future discontinuities to deliver strategic value

Businesses love trends.

Trends make life easier for planners, marketers and innovators because they provide the illusion of a safe framework to which they can attach their plans and initiatives. In a sense, trends do the hard yards by defining the domains for exploitation. Once this heavy lifting is done, it's then up to the skills of the business to exploit the obvious. The trouble is, all of your competitors are likely doing the same thing.

I first became aware of the corporate love for trends when I was appointed Consumer Insights Manager at Foster's. Charged with the responsibility for assisting marketing decisions including innovation, this role was my first real exposure to consumer and social trends. And I was soon able to see first-hand the influential and often central role that trends play in business decisions.

One of the first jobs in my new role was to develop a set of consumer trends that would act as a guiding framework for marketing and innovation—a corporate version of the ten commandments, if you like. After locking ourselves away for a couple of weeks, my colleagues and I came down from the mountain brandishing a list of trends that would surely take us to the promised land. We beamed with pride at what we thought was the originality of *our* trends and the creativity with which we had named each one: *Keeping it real* described the consumer's desire for authentic products and experiences. *Time as currency* captured the increasing value consumers placed on convenience due to a lack of time or energy. *Gender blending* spoke to the breaking down of traditional male and female stereotypes.

Little did we know, rather than place Foster's at the forefront of global innovation, what this set of trends actually did was to position us smack-bang in the middle of corporate mediocrity. Despite our initial hubris, you could be sure that every major consumer goods company in the world had a similar list of social trends guiding their marketing and innovation. Furthermore, our attachment to these trends only made us more vulnerable to more significant, less obvious changes emerging around us.

Trends are not enough

Trends essentially represent a noticeable shift—an emerging pattern of behaviour that is different from the established activities of society or an industry. To a business, trends often represent a change in the attitudes, preferences or behaviours of customers or consumers. As opposed to fads, which can come and go quickly, trends tend to be sustained, often representing fundamental shifts in the market.

And this is what makes trends important. Organisations must respond to trends or risk losing relevance with customers. This means constantly adapting what you do or how you do it to remain in harmony with evolving consumer preferences. At Foster's, the most senior management at the time even had a saying that was repeated throughout the company: 'The trend is your friend.' The message in this axiom was clear: *follow the trend*.

The danger, of course, is in relying too heavily on trends as a guide to the future.

The deceptive friend: *The comforting future-as-written impression provided by trends leaves many organisations unprepared for imminent discontinuities.*

It soon became apparent that trends also have significant limitations, especially with regard to their usefulness for (1) providing competitive advantage and (2) illuminating future market shifts.

1. **Trends don't provide competitive advantage.** The very fact that they are noticeable suggests there must be mounting and measurable evidence of change for a trend to exist. And this is the usefulness of trends: their visibility provides a guide for planning and innovation. But this visibility is also a weakness for organisations, because if we at Foster's were innovating to the latest social trends, then you could be sure our competitors were doing the same.

   The resulting convergent behaviour that trends promote is akin to moths being attracted to a flame. Pretty soon every player in the industry is innovating to the same reasoning, until a new norm is established. In this instance, trends rarely provide a competitive edge—unless you are the first to take advantage of them, in which case you'd be acting upon weaker signals. If all you are doing is responding to trends, then you're back with the pack.

2. **Trends are deceptive.** They convey a comforting *future-as-written* air that can provide the illusion of stability to all who worship at their altar. This comfort is deceiving because trends don't last. Sure, some trends last longer than others; some may even persist for decades and beyond. The future is never simply a linear continuation of the past, however, and sooner or later a significant discontinuity in the form of a fundamental market shift will emerge.

In today's world, these discontinuities are increasingly common and relying on trends fails to prepare you for their impact. Instead, a business-as-usual environment is assumed, and strategy is designed for an extrapolation of today's conditions (see figure 1.1). This lack of preparation for change is now your Achilles heel and inevitably leads to change being experienced as *disruption*—a significant shift in the organisation's operating environment for which you are unprepared. Examples of disruptive change are all too common today but few have been as public, as painful or as sudden as the crisis that enveloped the Australian live cattle export industry in 2011.

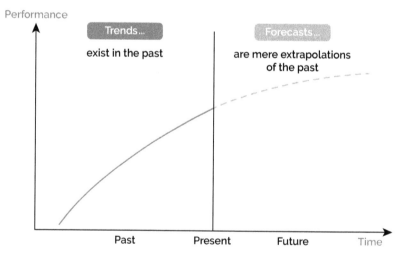

Figure 1.1: 'trends exist in the past'

My colleague Marcus Barber helped me to see trends in a new way by proposing that 'trends exist in the past'. So ingrained was our future-oriented view of trends that at first this observation seemed counterintuitive.

Before 2011 the industry had experienced a sustained period of growth in exports to Indonesia, a trend that was forecast to continue. However, in May 2011 the ABC's current affairs program *Four Corners* exposed cruelty inflicted on Australian cattle in Indonesian slaughterhouses. This led to a major public uproar and an immediate ban on abattoirs featured in the program, followed by a six-month ban on all live trade to Indonesia. The forecast growth trend, upon which industry members had based investment decisions worth millions of dollars, was immediately rendered worthless. Overnight the once prosperous industry was brought to its knees, and years later it was still trying to recover.

If the purpose of strategy is to exploit opportunities in order to achieve future goals, then the strategic value of information is in its capacity to illuminate plausible and significant future market shifts. It's within these shifts that new strategic opportunities reside, providing gateways to a step change in performance (see figure 1.2). Significant market shifts don't come along all that often; you want to be prepared for them when they do, and drive them when you can. If all you are doing is planning for a business-as-usual future, then 'the value of forecasts is very little'.[1]

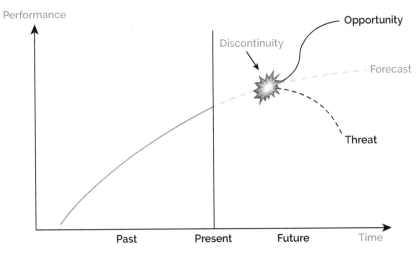

Figure 1.2: failing 'when they are needed most'[2]

Traditional forecasts fail to anticipate the significant market shifts that can deliver a step change in organisational performance. (Source: Adapted from Igor Ansoff.[3])

As the limitations of trends and forecasts as a source of insight into the future became clear, I realised there had to be more effective ways to approach strategy and innovation. Driven by an equal mix of curiosity and corporate competitiveness, I began to explore a question that would lead me to the emerging field of strategic foresight.

How do you get ahead of trends?

I wondered if it was possible to anticipate future market changes and strategic opportunities before they became obvious to competitors. And if so, how could I learn and apply such processes internally? At the same time, I came to the broader realisation that it wasn't just our use of trends that needed reviewing; our whole approach to information, strategy and innovation needed an overhaul.

Like many organisations over the preceding decades, Foster's had become an active and willing participant in the *information age*—an age in which businesses sought to acquire ever-greater amounts of market data in their pursuit of competitive advantage. The folly of this addiction to information was perfectly captured in comments from the Consumer Insights Manager at a large multinational firm with whom I worked several years later. Asked, 'What are the key challenges with internal data usage?', her reply was as universal as it was succinct:

- 'There is too much.'
- 'We don't use what we have.'
- 'They [internal staff] always want more.'

As for her Marketing Director, his great irritation was the fact that they had all this information yet never seemed to lead the market in innovation or to discover the 'next big thing'. I suspect this frustration is all too common.

Over the course of the information age we've seen the micro-analysis of company sales data; we've seen the collection of in-store scan data as a more accurate guide to consumption patterns; we've seen the explosion in market research and focus groups, with consumers being asked what they bought (ate, drank, did) last week, last month or in the past six months. Perhaps with *big data*, and its deceptively named accomplice, *predictive analytics*, we've now arrived at peak information.

In short, organisations have found more expensive and more intrusive ways of analysing their customers' current and past behaviours in a bid to succeed in the future. Given many of these same organisations continue to be surprised by significant market shifts, their actions suggest a kind of 'corporate madness'.

What's more, in many industries today we have the absurd situation where competitors spend millions of dollars to receive the same syndicated information from the same industry suppliers on the same day. The only winners in this scenario are the suppliers of the syndicated information. This reliance on mainstream information sources not only places individual organisations at risk of disruptive change, entire industries are in danger because of the convergent view of the future that this behaviour encourages.[4]

As for the effectiveness of such an approach, you can arrive at your own assessment by reflecting on the following:

1. Over the past decade, how much time, money or resources has your organisation spent acquiring and analysing information?
2. Over this same period, what have been the most significant changes or events to affect your industry?
3. And how many of your information sources or internal processes prepared you for these changes ahead of time?
4. Compared with your competitors, how distinct is your business strategy?

Inappropriate data usage

I'm not an opponent of traditional industry data sources. They clearly have important roles to play, including quantifying market size, monitoring company performance, testing product initiatives and assisting operational decisions. In fact, during my first nine years at Foster's I was as heavily involved in market analysis as anyone in the 100-plus-year history of the company. It wasn't until I moved into my new role as Foresight Manager and started using different methods to think about the future that I realised how consumed with data I/we had become. This reliance was so pervasive that we even incorporated the tag 'Consumer Led' into our corporate branding and everyday language, effectively formalising our reactionary relationship with the future. The withdrawal symptoms I suffered in my struggle to deprogram from this dependence were the corporate equivalent of going cold turkey.

What I *am* opposed to is inappropriate data usage, the practice of using types of information and processes for purposes beyond their capability—in this instance, the practice of using operational data for the strategic purpose of planning for the future. And here's my point: in today's turbulence, strategic insight into the future demands a purpose-built approach that is fit for the times. To settle for anything less condemns the organisation to a cycle of hope, shock and reaction.

There must be a better way!

If the fundamental challenges for business in the twenty-first century are environmental sensitivity, strategic transformation and strategic distinctiveness, then the purpose of information is clear if it is to deliver strategic value:

- It should enable decision makers to *reperceive* their future external environment—to see beyond business-as-usual and to anticipate future discontinuities.
- It should enable managers to *reconceive* the organisation's strategic positioning in order to exploit future opportunities and avoid possible threats.
- It should enable the organisation to thrive in times of turbulence, effectively turning market volatility to your competitive advantage.

To achieve these goals, information requires the following qualities:

- It should be specifically designed for, and oriented towards, the uncertainty of the future.
- It should allow managers to learn from the future, to exercise their strategic creativity and to form strategic judgements in the present.
- It should be generated from within the organisation so it is original and distinct.

Clearly, traditional information sources, with their external suppliers, syndicated access and emphasis on the past, are incapable of meeting the strategic needs of modern business.

And senior managers know this; it's the cause of great frustration. They see the amount of information they pay for; they see the number of internal analysts and planners employed to review this information; and they see the pile of reports, proposals and plans that come before them for approval. Yet for all this time, money and effort, they also see expensive innovation and investment ventures repeatedly fail; they see competitors consistently beating them to market with successful launches; and they feel the regular disruptive impact of unforeseen market shifts.

What these managers don't see is an alternative. They look to the future and feel overwhelmed by its uncertainty, its complexity, its vastness. And in their quiet moments they ask themselves, *Where do we start?*

In the absence of any obvious framework to navigate this perceived 'black hole', or any process to link learning about the future back to strategic initiatives, they return to the sources and processes they know, but no longer trust.

Yet such a framework and process does exist. And herein lies the great opportunity for every organisation: to adopt and integrate an approach to strategic design that specifically addresses the fundamental business challenges of the twenty-first century.

Scenario planning sits at the core of this approach.

PART II

LEARNING

CHAPTER 2

The latent resource

The business case for scenarios has never been stronger

World Expo 88 was a successful World's Fair hosted by the city of Brisbane over a six-month period in 1988. The theme of the Expo, *Leisure in the Age of Technology*, pointed to the optimism of the day when the pre-eminent conundrum was seen to be 'What are we going to do with all the free time technology will give us in the future?'

So how's that working out for you?

The idea of a reduced working week and increasing leisure time was hardly new, but in the late 1980s, when personal computers and mobile phones were about to go mainstream, the forecast of a leisure-rich future seemed entirely plausible. At least it did if you were simply to extrapolate from the rising influence of technology.

At the same time, however, an equally powerful force was emerging, one that when combined with technology would produce a cultural shift that contrasted sharply with the leisure-rich scenario imagined. That force was materialism.

With the growth of materialistic values came a culture of comparative consumption, instant gratification, debt, stress, insecurity and *increased* working hours. Personal identity became intertwined with material success—'I am what I own', 'I am what I earn', 'I am what I wear'. Perversely, over the next 20 years it was actually leisure time that was increasingly challenged as being busy ('busy-ness') assumed a form of social status. So rather than being the great facilitator of increased leisure, technology effectively played the role of a Trojan horse, enabling employees to videoconference 24/7 around the globe, to work from home on weekends, to answer work calls at night and to respond to emails while on holidays. 'Busy-ness in the Age of Technology' might have been a more appropriate Expo theme, although I acknowledge the potential marketing challenges.

In 1985 Alvin Toffler wrote:

I mistrust isolated trends, whether mini or mega. In a period of rapid change, strategic planning based on straight-line trend extrapolation is inherently treacherous...What is needed for planning is not a set of isolated trends, but multidimensional models that interrelate forces—technological, social, political, even cultural, along with economics.[1]

The utopian future foretold at World Expo 88 presents as the classic oversimplification that occurs when forces for change are viewed in isolation and their effects extrapolated linearly. Overcoming this linear perspective requires a systemic approach, one that recognises the interconnected and interactive nature of forces as drivers of change.

Introducing scenarios

Scenarios are detailed descriptions or stories of plausible future events and outcomes. They are stories 'in the sense that they describe the evolving dynamics of interacting forces rather than the static picture of a single end-point future'.[2] The word itself derives from the performing arts where scenarios historically provided the supporting background to a scene. These scenarios would be pinned to the back scenery as a reference for the actors, outlining the broad plot and its series of actions and events. Today scenarios in business serve a similar purpose: they provide a backdrop or framework for decision making.

In a business setting, scenarios are used to generate and explore the different future environments in which an organisation may have to operate. These hypothetical backgrounds allow the organisation to consider its strategic positioning and objectives from different, future contexts. Scenario planning, then, is the process of developing strategic responses to these alternative futures.

The purpose of scenarios is not to predict the future or to get the future right, but rather to enable better decisions today,[3] to empower organisations to shape the future they want. Ultimately, they are a learning and reframing tool, providing learning about the drivers of change and their possible impacts, while helping you to form new perspectives on the future and your organisation's role within it.

Scenarios in business: a mixed history

The history of scenarios in business makes for an interesting scenario itself. It's a story that features larger-than-life individuals, a mysterious, little-known Frenchman, a corporate success of mythical proportions, a brief period as the latest management fad, and the inevitable 'fade away' that seems to follow overnight celebrity. It's an intriguing history, with its own inflection points and discontinuities, as one might expect of an intuitive process specifically designed to deal with future uncertainty.

The application of scenarios in business has its genesis in the political uncertainty following World War II. US defence projects were understandably still high on government agendas and the challenge of how, and where, to focus their defence budget was a complex issue. In order to make sound judgements about their spending, departments needed to gain insights into the future political environments in which their weapons might need to be used. This uncertainty provided the platform for scenario thinking to emerge. Consequently, the US Department of Defense engaged the RAND Corporation to help it decide which projects should be funded for the development of new weapons systems.[4]

If scenario planning has a patriarch, then it was surely the larger-than-life Herman Kahn. Working for the RAND Corporation, Kahn began developing scenarios for the US Air Defense System Missile Command and he became known for *thinking the unthinkable*.[5] He would later recall,

We deliberately chose the word [scenario] to deglamorize the concept. In writing the scenarios for various situations we kept saying 'Remember, it's only a scenario', the kind of thing that is produced by Hollywood writers.[6]

In particular, his work highlighted the extreme and dire consequences of nuclear war.[7] Rather than claiming to forecast the future, Kahn's scenarios were exploratory and intended to get people thinking about the future, to help overcome the 'social inhibitions which reinforce natural tendencies to avoid thinking about unpleasant subjects'.[8]

While Herman Kahn was developing scenarios for the US military in the 1950s and 1960s, the Western world was going through a period of sustained and steady economic growth that lasted until the early 1970s. 'Foresightful' businesses, however, were aware that the good times couldn't last forever. In the late 1960s the oil giant Shell began exploring the long-term future. Heading up these early explorations, and inspired by the approach of Herman Kahn, were Ted Newland in London and Pierre Wack in Paris.

They were just in time. In the 1970s, as Western economies stagnated and inflation rose, traditional forecasting techniques proved increasingly unreliable and ineffective, rocking the confidence of business managers. The uncertainty of the times demanded another approach to forward planning. The moment had arrived for scenario planning to be embraced by the business world.

Global demand for oil had risen consistently since the end of the war, and it was assumed that this trend would continue. So Wack and Newland focused their attention on the supply side. Assuming the mindsets of industry stakeholders, and roleplaying their likely responses, Wack could see that consistency of supply was not guaranteed going forward: 'If we were Iran, we would do the same,' he said.[9] The scenario process had allowed him to foresee developments that others had not yet considered.

After presenting their scenarios to senior management, Wack was handed the task of giving presentations to Shell's operating managers around the world. 'Be careful!' he warned exploration and production managers. 'You are about to lose the major part of your mining rents.' 'Prepare!' he advised oil refiners and marketers. 'You are about to become a low-growth industry.'[10]

And slowly behaviour at Shell did begin to change. Where previously executives did not have to consider the consequences of overinvestment, now Shell managers began to implement more adaptable and 'frugal' practices informed by their internal 'energy crisis' scenario.[11]

The planners had hit paydirt. In 1973 the scenario became a reality when the Yom Kippur War led to political embargos limiting the supply of oil to several countries, and oil prices rose fivefold. Pierre Wack's work had done enough to ensure strategic preparation for such an event. 'Emotionally prepared for the change', Shell responded well ahead of its competitors and as a result rose from seventh to second on the profitability league table of oil companies.[12] The economic value of being well prepared was calculated to be in the billions of dollars.[13]

In the world of scenarios, Shell's success in the early 1970s is the stuff of legend. In fact, Shell has become something of a beacon in the field of scenario planning, producing a steady roll call of influential strategists, scenario planners and storytellers. A review of the literature on scenarios shows the proficiency of Shell alumni, dominated by pioneers like Wack[14][15], Beck[16], Schwartz[17], van der Heijden[18], de Geus[19], Jaworski[20] and Schoemaker.[21]

To this day Shell remains the standard-bearer in scenario planning, regularly producing a new set of global scenarios to guide the group's strategic direction. From the Chief Executive down, these scenarios are communicated to all Shell employees, promoting a shared sense of environmental understanding and directional purpose. Shell's holistic strategy development process, with its integration of global scenarios and group strategy, remains the corporate model for others to aspire to.

Golden years

Following Shell's success, and meeting the need for a more effective planning method for turbulent times, scenarios basked in the corporate sun throughout the 1970s. A 1981 study of European companies by Pentti Malaska found that 88 per cent of the firms that were using scenario planning had started to do so only after the first oil shock of 1973.[22] Studies by Linneman and Klein looking at the extent of scenario usage among corporations in 1977 and 1981 indicated that the method was being rapidly adopted. In fact, according to estimates based on their research, half the US Fortune 1000 industrial firms in the early 1980s were using scenario techniques in their planning process.[23] [24]

Despite this heady beginning, it's fair to say that the use of scenarios in business has not maintained its growth trajectory over the past 40 years. And where scenarios are applied, often their format bears little resemblance to the process introduced by Pierre Wack and his colleagues at Shell.

Perhaps overall the history of scenarios in business is defined by underachievement, their lack of impact underpinned by an enduring 'identity crisis' that continues to prevent scenarios from driving business strategy and innovation as they should. Instead, scenarios remain a somewhat fuzzy and largely misunderstood concept. Even today, most corporate managers would struggle to answer the most basic questions about scenarios: *What are they? What is their purpose? How do you create them? How do you use them? What can they do for me?*

And until these questions can be answered consistently, prospective scenario planners will continue to have just the one famous success from 1973 to point to in support of their claim, 'Look, it does work!'

A second coming?

The research of Malaska, Linneman and Klein supports the logic of a correlation between the usage of scenarios and perceived environmental volatility. If this is the case, then today's uncertainty provides the opportunity for scenarios once again to be recognised as an idea whose time has come. And it's true, scenarios are enjoying a resurgence in public interest judging by the increased number of publications and available public works.[25][26]

Suitable conditions might be enough to get the scenario foot in the planning door; however, the ongoing perceived value of the scenarios has not been sufficient to maintain this footing once conditions stabilised. So if the current intellectual interest in scenarios is to translate into sustained corporate adoption, then scenarios must overcome the misperceptions and hurdles that have plagued their effectiveness thus far, namely:

- Scenarios are not taken seriously.
- Scenarios are complex.
- Scenario benefits are too far away.
- Scenarios take too long.
- .Scenarios lack consistency.
- Scenarios are not integrated.

SCENARIOS ARE NOT TAKEN SERIOUSLY

When I put forward my proposal to the Managing Director at Foster's for a new role specifically focused on the future, my original job title suggestion was Environmental Scanning Manager. My recommendation was quite intentional: I wanted the role to be taken seriously, so I deliberately avoided the words *futurist* or *foresight*. It wasn't to be, though, and later that month I became the group's inaugural Foresight Manager.

In the eyes of my (half-serious?) colleagues I was now the resident fortune teller, palm reader, crystal ball gazer (insert cliché of choice here).

The truth behind their jibes points to one of the reasons for the lack of scenario usage in business: serious attempts to understand the future are confused with efforts to predict, and since prediction isn't possible, scenarios are either dismissed as an exercise in futility or else just not taken seriously.[27] 'Can't predict, so why bother?' seems to be the attitude, as those who carry the futurist title are regarded with a scepticism usually reserved for snake oil salesmen.

The other factor undermining the use of scenarios is the association of the future with fantasy and science fiction, something the cartoon series *The Jetsons* has a lot to answer for. Before a scenario planning project with the multinational Kraft I sat in a briefing with internal managers and some representatives from an external marketing agency. After explaining that we were about to enter a two-day scenarios workshop to explore how consumer behaviours and needs might evolve over the next 10 years, one of the marketers deadpanned, 'Is that where you make up stories about flying cars and robot maids?' He wasn't trying to be funny; he just had very little idea about scenarios. In his mind anything to do with the future just had to involve flying cars, right?

SCENARIOS ARE COMPLEX

Scenarios can be complex because they take time. They're complex because they involve many variables. They're complex because they require intensive research. They're complex because they're intuitive, subjective and qualitative. They're complex because they involve imagining circumstances that don't yet exist. And they're complex because they explicitly deal with uncertainty, providing alternatives to provoke answers, rather than the answers themselves.

Yet leaders prefer the illusion of certainty. It allows them to act quickly and decisively, to convey perceptions of control. 'Just give me a number,' they plead[28], preferring to outsource judgement rather than exercising their own. To those conditioned to receiving serious information in tables and graphs[29], the qualitative nature of scenarios can appear lightweight, not grounded in reality and merely adding to the 'noise'.

From the resultant impasse between manager and methodology, between certainty and uncertainty, simplicity and perceived complexity, scenarios rarely emerge a winner.

SCENARIO BENEFITS ARE TOO FAR AWAY

Scenarios, particularly longer-term scenarios, are victims of the short-term agendas driven by organisations and their key stakeholders. With CEOs being rewarded for achieving annual targets, shareholders demanding higher dividends, and governments seeking re-election every three or four years, it's little wonder initiatives with a longer-term focus are rarely stamped 'Urgent'.

We see this short-termism in the following exchange between then Victorian premier John Brumby and 3AW Melbourne radio announcer Neil Mitchell in 2008. To provide some context, Victoria had been suffering from a long drought and its residents had been on water restrictions for several years. The two men are discussing the merits of building another dam to help support Victoria's water supply.

John Brumby: People say, gee, why didn't you build a dam? You know the Thomson Dam [Melbourne's biggest] was, from the time it was announced to the time it filled, was 14 years.

So, if people say, 'Well, where's the dam today?' it should have been built when Jeff Kennett was Premier. [Jeff Kennett led the previous state government from 1992 to 1999.]

People say, 'Build a dam', as if that's going to fix the problem tomorrow. It's not.

Neil Mitchell: But will it fix the future, help the future?

John Brumby: What, 12 or 14 years away? . . . We're talking about problems now.

Regardless of the rights or wrongs of building another dam, what stands out in this conversation is the former premier's attitude towards the future. His argument is not that he doesn't want another dam; rather, he has an issue with the length of time it takes to build that dam. Inside corporations this attitude translates to: 'We're too busy dealing with today's realities to worry about tomorrow's possibilities; the future can look after itself'. Within this culture of immediacy scenarios suffer from a perceived lack of relevance to today's business priorities. The result is an ongoing cycle of crises and crisis management, as the company is forced to cope with the inconvenient arrival of unconsidered futures.

And it's true, within this operating context of *immediacy*, scenario benefits are absolutely too far away. The whole purpose of scenarios is to do the thinking and planning *before* the horse has bolted. Somewhat counterintuitively, the best time to undertake a scenario process is when there is no pressing need, when operating conditions are relatively stable. Note that these were the circumstances enjoyed by the oil industry prior to the 1972 Shell scenarios. In all likelihood, if scenarios had been originally proposed at Shell *after* the 1973 oil crisis they would never have been endorsed. Stability offers the luxuries of time and clarity of mind, both essential to the corporate benefits that then flow from a successful scenario planning exercise.

SCENARIOS TAKE TOO LONG

'Hi Steve, we're holding an upcoming conference / workshop / planning retreat. The theme is *Building Better Futures / Winning the Future / Innovating for the Future*...

'We'd like you to facilitate a session looking at the next 10 years for our industry and the strategic opportunities for our company — it's a very important session.

'Oh, and can you do this within three hours?'

Such a request will be familiar to anyone who has consulted in the field of scenario planning. It reveals that while there might be a corporate appetite for understanding the future, rarely is this matched with a willingness to invest the time needed. In some respects, this focus on the here and now is almost childlike.

In the early 1970s psychologist Walter Mischel led a series of studies at Stanford University on delayed gratification that became known as the Stanford marshmallow experiment.[30] In these studies, children aged three to five were offered a choice between receiving one small reward immediately (a marshmallow, a cookie or a pretzel), or two small rewards if they waited 15 minutes. Of the 600 participants, only one-third were able to control their desires long enough to get the larger reward.

Subsequent studies found that children who were willing to wait for what they wanted tended to achieve better long-term outcomes in terms of test scores, education levels, and physical health.

Just like small children, managers often struggle with delayed gratification. Their desire for the immediate 'sugar hit' consistently overrides their quest for better long-term outcomes: 'Scenarios take too long. We need a strategy [or a new product] now, not in six months' time.' But this corporate impatience, exhibited in the form of a short-term, myopic focus, comes at a price.

Ongoing strategic surprises ensure organisations are so busy responding to unforeseen external changes that they rarely give themselves the opportunity to think seriously about the broader or longer-term future. With their focus on putting out the latest 'fire', or meeting the next short-term target, it's no wonder many exist in a state of 'temporal exhaustion'.[31] As sociologist Elise Boulding correctly diagnosed, if one is mentally out of breath all the time from dealing with the present, there is no energy left for imagining the future[32] (see figure 2.1, overleaf).

The result of this temporal exhaustion is inefficiency in the form of wasted time, money and resources. In effect, the organisation chooses to take the indirect route to the future, unaware of what's ahead, unsure of where it's going and without due consideration of the consequences of its decisions. In this respect, companies tend to approach the future much like a sailing boat tacking into the wind, lurching from one idea to the next, in a constant cycle of doing, undoing and redoing (see figure 2.2, overleaf).

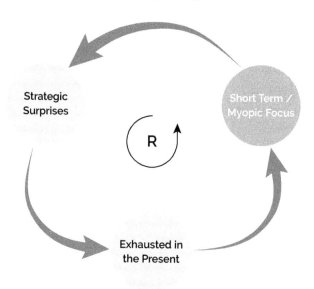

Figure 2.1: an exhausting reinforcing loop

Ignoring a broader or longer-term outlook, organisations can exist in a state of perpetual firefighting, constantly responding to strategic surprises.

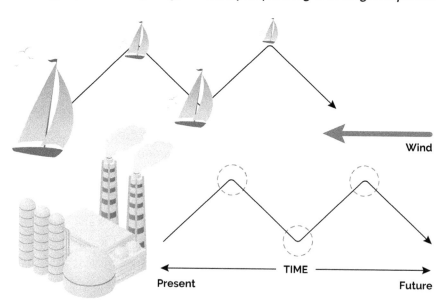

Figure 2.2: where are we headed?

Much like a sailing boat heading upwind, organisations tend to 'tack' their way into the future through an inefficient cycle of doing, undoing and redoing.

Yes, scenarios take time. But the new perceptions generated by this process are the reward for your patience. They deliver a clarity about the future that alleviates your exhaustion in the present, helping you to act with confidence and a cohesive purpose. Informed from a new perspective, the organisation minimises resource-wasting deviations and externally imposed disruptions as it takes the more direct route to the future (see figure 2.3).

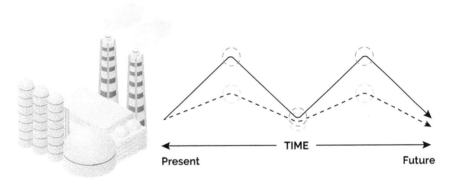

Figure 2.3: taking a more direct route to the future

Scenarios optimise performance by flattening out inefficient deviations, thereby freeing up resources to invest in strategic thinking and innovation.

While scenarios take time, they also actually save time—and better still, they *optimise* time. To borrow from futurist Joel Barker, 'Speed is useful only if you are running in the right direction'.[33] Effective scenarios point you in the right direction.

SCENARIOS LACK CONSISTENCY

'In my experience,' observes former Shell employee Napier Collyns, 'scenario planning is an interpretive practice—it's really closer to magic than technique…Look long enough, hard enough, and the pieces will fall into place.'[34]

Developing scenarios is often referred to as an art, rather than a science. It's an intuitive practice that can produce surprising results, not a linear process where conclusions are obvious or predetermined.

And it's this intuitive aspect that provides their strategic advantage. Internally generated scenarios produce a corporate asset in the form of a unique perspective of the future that cannot be replicated by competitors.

But this intuitive trait is also a weakness. It means that there are almost as many ways of building and planning with scenarios as there are practitioners.[35] It also means that the field is characterised by inconsistency and confusion. Reliance on intuition also implies that benefits can't be assured—scenarios don't come with a *money-back guarantee*. As a result, the experience can often leave a hollow feeling in its wake. And it's little wonder. Read plenty of books on scenarios and you will emerge with a vague understanding of the broad process. That's the easy part. Much harder to achieve is an original insight into the future that leads to better decisions—the critical measure of scenario success. Insights don't just appear in the final chapter of the literature; scenarios are not a colour-by-numbers exercise.

Thus, their intuitive aspect ensures that the pointy-end value of scenarios relies as much on the skills of the personnel involved as it does on the process itself. And this causes ongoing wariness among managers who are averse to 'magic' in the workplace and seek nothing more than consistency and guaranteed performance when choosing how best to allocate their budgets and resources.

SCENARIOS ARE NOT INTEGRATED

From my experience, the main reason scenarios fail to gain a solid footing within organisations is a lack of integration both with internal strategy and innovation processes, and with managerial priorities.

Instead, when they are used, scenarios are often trialled as stand-alone activities, sitting outside internally established strategy and innovation processes. With the best of intentions, the future is explored, scenarios are developed, insights might be gained, and then...*nothing*. Typically, the lack of integration with other recognised processes condemns these forays to novel, one-off episodes. 'We tried that—it was interesting, but nothing came of it,' declare frustrated managers, as the future is cast off as a creative indulgence for less urgent times.

In the absence of this integration, managers rightly question the value of scenarios around three key criteria:

- **relevance**—'How will they address our concerns?'
- **usage**—'What do we do with the output?'
- **impact**—'What benefits will they deliver?'

From personal experience, it's clear that scenarios must be linked back to organisational strategy and innovation if they are to prove either useful or sustainable. So, on the surface at least, it appears that the long-term success of scenarios relies on this level of integration. However, to assume that this dependence operates in one direction only is to seriously understate the empowering capacity of scenarios.

On the contrary, the relationship is co-dependent; if anything, in a turbulent environment the long-term success of the organisation relies more on scenario integration than the other way around. It is simply not enough for scenarios to be integrated into, or to sit alongside, established company processes; scenarios should *drive* strategic planning and innovation. They are fundamental to future business success (see figure 2.4).

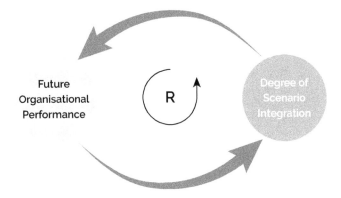

Figure 2.4: mutual dependence

Integration with internal processes is essential for scenarios to be successful and fundamental to future business performance in a turbulent environment.

CHAPTER 3

Where does the future fit?

Scenarios should drive strategic thinking and innovation

In 2011 I was invited to speak at the annual conference for a company offering development and support services to a vast network of business advisers across Australia. This organisation had been operating successfully for almost 20 years, providing business tools and strategy methodologies to advance the capabilities of their members. It was exposure to one of these methods during the conference that reinforced for me how the future remains the essential missing element in strategy.

On a handout given to each attendee was a model for how to take a business from where it is now to where it wants to be. This approach was accompanied by the diagram represented in figure 3.1 (overleaf) and the following three questions:

1. How is your business performing NOW?
2. What is your vision for WHERE you want to take your business?
3. What are your key strategies as to HOW you will get there?

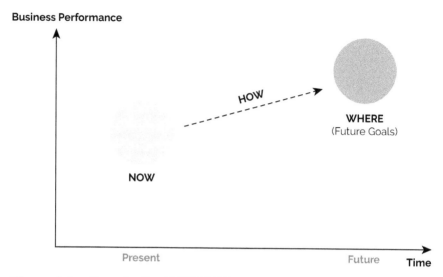

Figure 3.1: where is the 'WHERE'?

Most strategies take the future for granted, assuming future conditions will be similar to those of today, and presenting the achievement of future goals as a fait accompli.

Which begs the question: *Just where is the 'WHERE'?* What are the different future contexts or conditions in which your goals might have to be achieved?

Not that this particular organisation is uniquely guilty of this oversight. The fact is that the future remains largely absent from most strategic thinking, and business plans are largely hatched as if the organisation operates within a bubble.

What informs your strategy?

There are many definitions of strategy, and to varying degrees most of these touch on the concepts of goals, directions, pathways and plans, yet very few explicitly focus on the central role of the future, or rather our *perceptions* of the future. Most therefore underplay the critical relationship between the goals being set, the strategies being developed and the future environments in which these strategies might be played out.

Instead, by simply presenting strategy as 'a path to get from here to there'[1], plausible changes in the business environment are either ignored or taken for granted. The illusion of managerial control and future certainty is propagated, as the achievement of corporate goals is falsely presented as a *fait accompli*; as long as management can get its planning right (HOW), everything will be fine. Serious consideration is rarely given to the changed future conditions in which these goals might have to be achieved, or even whether the goals will remain legitimate in light of these changed conditions (see figure 3.2).

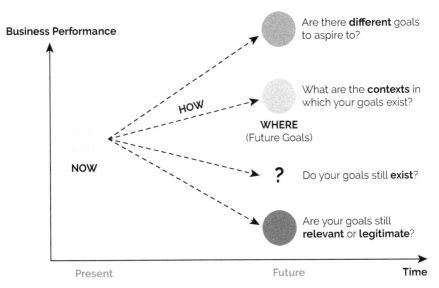

Figure 3.2: a fluid landscape

Since all strategies are played out in the arena of the future, serious consideration should be applied to understanding the different contexts that will ultimately determine strategic success.

The results of this strategic oversight are the high rates of corporate failure resulting from what Pierre Wack termed a 'crisis of perception'.[3] Crises of perception occur when companies get the future wrong, or, more particularly, when they are not *seeing* correctly. After retiring from Shell, Wack delivered seminars in which he would challenge his audience:

> **Look back at your company, ten years back. And look at the picture of the environment they had at the time. Try to see it with the most possible detail. And then you know what happened. And you see there was probably a crisis of perception. The company at the time could not see things which were seeable.[4]**

Putting the future in its place

'Futurists don't study "the future" because "the future" does not exist,' suggests futurist Jim Dator. 'What does exist and what can and should be studied are "images of the future" which each person has, and which form the basis for individual and collective acts in the present which then impact upon "the future".'[2] Building on this logic, a holistic definition for strategy emerges:

Strategy is a *plan for action* to achieve *your goals* in *perceived future environments*.

Scenario planning places our perceptions of the future at the core of strategy development. It takes a holistic view of strategy development that recognises the three essential components of strategic design:

1. **Your goals**
   - Identity—how the organisation *sees* itself
   - Vision—what the organisation wants to *achieve*
2. **Perceived future environments**
   - Contexts for future goals and actions
3. **A plan for action**
   - *What* the organisation will do
   - *How* it will do it.

This definition of strategy positions scenarios as the central component of strategic planning by emphasising the need to understand perceived future environments. These perceptions then form the organisation's *strategic reasoning*, underpinning the logic of its strategic positioning and strategic objectives — *why* you do what you do.

More specifically, and much more importantly, scenarios provide managers with *their* strategic reasoning — an original perspective on the future. The way *they* now see the future will reflect the drivers *they* feel are significant, the storylines *they* feel are important and the creative input of *their* internal staff. This unique view of the future is the birthplace of strategic distinctiveness.

The expression *perceived future environments* is both deliberate and significant. First, it acknowledges that the future exists as images or perceptions in our mind; there are no facts about the long-term future. Second, the uncertainty and openness of the future is acknowledged in the plural 'environments'.

These points provide important guides for successful strategic design in that they calibrate the focus away from accumulating external facts towards interrogating internal mental models (*perceptions*), and away from accepting singular forecasts to exploring multiple scenarios (*future environments*). It's this exploration of multiple future environments that brings scenarios to the fore in strategic design.

Why scenarios?

The use of scenarios is based on the philosophy that the best way to improve decisions is to improve understanding about the future. And as a tool for understanding and anticipating future conditions of strategic significance, the scenario method is unsurpassed. In this respect, scenarios satisfy the criteria for strategically valuable information outlined on pages 10 and 11.

SCENARIOS ARE PURPOSE-BUILT FOR UNCERTAINTY

Multiple scenarios acknowledge the uncertainty of the future. The overwhelming logic for using scenarios in strategic planning is articulated well by two of the pioneers in the field. For Pierre Wack, 'Decision makers facing uncertain situations have a right to know just how uncertain they are. Accordingly, it is essential to try to put as much light on critical uncertainties as on the predetermined elements.'[5] Ian Wilson adds, 'The inevitable consequence of this fact is that strategy should be the product not of a single-point forecast but of a set of alternative futures that explore these uncertainties.'[6]

Scenarios differ from forecasts in giving visibility to uncertainty. By outlining plausible future events and outcomes, managers gain transparency to support their decision making. Whereas forecasts conceal uncertainty, scenarios reveal it.

SCENARIOS ARE HOLISTIC

Scenarios acknowledge that trends don't act in isolation and that the future is not linear. Multiple factors influence the business environment concurrently; they interact with one another to produce surprising outcomes.

This recognition of systemic interaction is a key differential between scenarios and other methods such as SWOT analysis, stand-alone scanning exercises and trends analysis. These more common approaches tend to simplify the future by treating forces in isolation, merely extrapolating their individual impact rather than looking for the emergent properties that result from their interaction.

SCENARIOS ENABLE STRATEGIC JUDGEMENTS

Scenarios provide a more complete, systemic picture of future outcomes. Just as trends don't act in isolation, nor are the effects of change felt in isolation. Scenarios acknowledge the interconnected nature of the broader contextual environment in which an organisation operates, and explore this interdependence when describing future impacts of events and forces.

It's this fuller picture of the future provided by scenarios that enables managers to form strategic judgements with greater confidence.

SCENARIOS UNLOCK STRATEGIC CREATIVITY

Scenarios facilitate the perceptual and conceptual shifts necessary for strategic transformation in a turbulent environment. Through disciplined exploration of the future, scenarios enable managers to foresee different future contexts in which the organisation might have to operate, helping to formulate new strategic reasoning that is a better match with 'reality as it is, and reality as it is going to be'.[7]

In this respect, scenarios perform the role of an alchemist; they are the maypole around which the organisation's strategic positioning and objectives interact and evolve. This is why scenarios should drive strategic thinking and innovation.

This holistic approach to strategy, in which scenarios sit at the core, reframes strategic design as the organisation's principal creative and learning activity.

CHAPTER 4

Reframing strategy

Strategic design is the organisation's principal creative and learning activity

Organisations are poor at strategy. They treat it as an afterthought, something they'll get to when time permits. Or else it's an incremental planning exercise, a dour number-crunching routine or an inconvenient obligation that just has to be done.

Of course, if you have these feelings of indifference or even disdain towards strategy, then you're hardly going to invest any more time and resources into the process than you feel are necessary. Instead, the go-to approach for many businesses resembles the following:

- A two-day planning retreat is scheduled offsite for a select group of the organisation's most senior personnel. It helps if these people are avid golfers, as a golf course is a usual prerequisite for the chosen location.

- Pre-reading is gathered tirelessly by junior analysts who either won't be invited to the workshop or if they are will play only a supporting role.

- Three days prior to the workshop, the pre-reading is distributed. This usually consists of voluminous reports (which only the junior analysts have had time to digest) bound in a corporate-branded folder so thick any federal court lawyer would be proud to call it their own. (I once received a pre-read email containing 27 different attachments just 36 hours before the workshop.) These notes are almost never read owing to a lack of time (sorry, analysts!).

- On the evening of the first day away energy levels are high. Progress has been made on the strategic plan and we're all relaxed away from home for the night—time to let our hair down with a few drinks.

- On the afternoon of the second day energy has sagged. People are tired from the night before and their thoughts turn to heading home early so they can beat the traffic. 'Let's get this over and done with.'

- Back at work an email is sent around thanking everyone for their contribution and spruiking the great output. Then . . .

- *Nothing.* Everyone's back to being busy and the only lasting conversation is likely to revolve around the events of the evening away.

- But that's okay, because 'Here it is. We've done our strategy!'

It's hardly surprising, then, that organisations continue to be blindsided by unforeseen change when their strategy processes have been reduced to this cliché, focused on output rather than learning, creativity and originality.

Companies adopt this approach because they don't know any different. It's an approach that results from a number of misconceptions that continue to limit the role and influence of strategy within organisations, namely:

Strategy is planning

Strategy is not planning. Strategic design is about setting the organisation's future direction and goals. It involves two significant creative steps:

1. reperceiving the future business environment
2. reconceiving the organisation's role within these different futures.

Strategising is about perception and conception. It requires imagination, creativity, innovation and entrepreneurialism.

Planning, on the other hand, is about doing and getting things done. It's about operations and implementation. Planning requires a different set of attributes: attention to detail, adherence to process and budgetary constraints. Planning is about operating within the broader context of the directional strategy; it is downstream from strategising.

Strategist Gary Hamel makes his distinction between planning and strategising pretty clear.[1] He argues that,

Planning is about programming, not discovering. Planning is for technocrats, not dreamers. Giving planners responsibility for creating strategy is like asking a bricklayer to create Michelangelo's *Pieta*.

And this distinction between planning and strategic design is crucial. It sets the tone for how, and by whom, strategy is developed. In the absence of such a distinction, strategic processes and participants continue to be misaligned with purpose, with the output simply reinforcing the dour stereotype of strategy and strategists.

Strategy is dour

When strategy isn't differentiated from planning, it is viewed as a dry, serious and arduous activity that focuses on number-crunching, data tables and forecasts. It then follows that the people best equipped to perform such roles are those with skills in such activities. And this is what many strategy teams resemble.

There's an unspoken belief in business that the development of strategy is the domain of some exclusive club, best carried out by the organisation's 'best and brightest' behind closed doors. These people are chosen because of their industry experience or their MBA qualifications or, in the ultimate snub to strategy, because they just don't *fit* in any other department.

What is obviously missing from this approach is an appreciation of the creative aspect of strategy development. While the process might be rigorous and appear sound on a spreadsheet, it is seldom likely to produce more than incremental strategic changes, the proverbial 'last year plus 5 per cent improvement'. In a volatile environment, where the organisation needs to regenerate its strategic outlook, creativity should always take precedence over a dour, financially driven approach.

Strategy is output

When strategy development is viewed as a dour and incremental affair it often takes on an output focus, where the aim is simply to get the job done, to produce a document. It's even seen as an inconvenient interruption to the real work of day-to-day activities—'This is something we just have to get through'. Companies that focus on producing output in order to meet their internal obligations are most likely to adhere to the clichéd approach to strategy development outlined earlier.

It's time to rethink strategy

In turbulent times, the purpose of strategic design is to generate a new and distinct strategic outlook that is *fit* for the future. In this environment, strategy development cannot be accepted as some obligatory exercise in incrementalism best performed by number crunchers behind closed doors. Instead, strategic design calls on the skills of creative and innovative thinkers, people with the imagination to conceive future change and the entrepreneurial ability to apply meaning to the organisation. Indeed, strategic design is the organisation's principal creative and learning activity; it is the foundation of corporate entrepreneurship and innovation (see figure 4.1).

Figure 4.1: layers of organisational creativity and innovation

Strategic design, the process of generating a new and distinct strategic outlook, is the foundation of corporate entrepreneurship and innovation.

Reframing strategy as a creative learning exercise in turn reconceives it as a *process-oriented* activity, rather than an *output-oriented* one. From this viewpoint, the purpose of strategic design is no longer to satisfy the internal requirement for a new document every three or four years. And rather than being done under sufferance, strategy formulation should be embraced with the same enthusiasm as any other creative or innovative exercise.

Strategic principles

The perception of strategic design as a creative learning activity is founded on five interconnected principles:

1. **Strategy as resource**: An original strategic outlook that is *fit* for the future is the organisation's ultimate asset—its key to a sustained competitive edge.

2. **Strategy as process**: In times of turbulence, organisations need to regenerate their strategic outlook to remain in harmony with the external environment.

3. **Strategy as creativity**: Creative thinking is necessary for reperceiving future environments and reconceiving future

strategic responses. Strategic creativity takes precedence over financially driven strategic development.

4. **Strategy as learning**: Understanding the forces driving future change and their plausible impacts is the key to unlocking strategic creativity.

5. **Strategy as participation**: Participatory strategy development is essential for organisational learning and strategy execution.

Let me explain each principle in further detail.

1. STRATEGY AS RESOURCE

An all-encompassing strategic outlook represents the organisation's holistic view of its future external and internal environment, its *strategic reasoning, positioning* and *objectives* (see figure 4.2). Such an outlook is the organisation's unique fingerprint.

1. Your goals
- Identity — how the organisation *sees* itself
- Vision — what the organisation wants to *achieve*

2. Perceived future environments
- *Contexts* for future goals and actions

3. A plan for action
- *What* the organisation will do
- *How* it will do it

Strategic Positioning

Strategic Reasoning

Strategic Objectives

Strategic Outlook

Figure 4.2: the organisation's fingerprint

The all-encompassing strategic outlook is a corporate asset that cannot be replicated.

Competitors may be able to respond to what you do, but they can never know the intricacies of your strategic reasoning—*how* you're seeing the future environment, and *why*. This is why your strategic outlook is such a corporate asset. The quality of this strategic resource is ultimately determined by:

- strategic *fit* with future reality
- strategic *differentiation* from competitors
- strategic *execution*.

Improvement in business performance begins with taking a resource-based view of strategy. Such a view values the company's strategic outlook in the same light as its more tangible assets — its people, products, infrastructure, distribution networks and finances. In fact, given that the acquisition, development and use of other resources springs from this perspective, the strategic outlook sits alone as the corporation's ultimate asset.

Once it is reframed as a resource, the folly of treating your strategy as the product of a weekend retreat, or as the private domain of a select few, becomes obvious. Instead, like any valuable resource, strategy requires ongoing investment. It requires time and energy for development, resources for support and a process for optimal outcomes.

2. STRATEGY AS PROCESS

It's generally accepted that the essential activities of management are 'decision making' and 'problem solving'.[2] Indeed, senior management is the reward for consistently good judgement. So why do these same senior executives remain notoriously poor at foreseeing or responding to significant changes in their business environment?

One argument is that managers have different skill sets from strategists, that their superior decision-making skills are incongruent with the creative aptitudes necessary to design strategies for the future. But I don't agree. Decision making, like creativity, relies on forming a judgement based on stimulus. The problem lies not with the tradesman, but with the tools.

When managers hear the word *process* their thoughts instantly turn to innovation gridlock, red tape, inaction and the like. 'Only bureaucracies have processes!' they insist. And it's true, processes can stifle creativity and action. They can certainly test your patience. But just as often this perception of *process as straitjacket* is derived from the temporal exhaustion and need for instant fixes that result from a lack of corporate foresight—'We need a new product/strategy now!' (refer to the section 'Scenario benefits are too far away' on page 23). No process, no matter how efficient, will survive the demands of such suffocating urgency.

It doesn't have to be this way. In fact, information overload and increasing business volatility have created the conditions in which internal processes have never been more important. And just as strategy should be viewed as an internal resource, so your process for designing strategy should be considered a dynamic capability delivering strategic value that is difficult to imitate.[3] In particular, an internal strategy process becomes a valuable corporate asset when it unlocks latent or constrained business potential by enabling:

- better decision making (*reperceiving, reconceiving*)
- original decision making (*creativity, differentiation*)
- faster decision making (*learning, understanding*)
- effective decision making (*participation, implementation*)
- cohesive decision making (*consistency, purposeful*)
- earlier decision making (*sensitivity, interpretation*).

Contrary to popular belief, these outcomes are not restricted to 'sexy', smaller start-ups seemingly unrestricted by process. Size doesn't matter. It's not the lack of process that enables entrepreneurs to seize opportunities earlier; it's their lack of attachment to 'what is' and their ability to detect significance in weaker signals of change. Properly executed strategic processes are about unlocking entrepreneurial potential, not suppressing it.

For an organisation investing in strategic design, this means embedding a process that is:

- creative, learning-based and participatory
  - enables fresh perspectives to emerge on the external and internal environments, allowing managers to *reperceive* their future business environment and to *reconceive* the organisation's strategic position within these future environments (*better* decision making)
  - harnesses the latent knowledge and creativity of internal staff to develop an original and differentiated strategic outlook (*original* decision making)
  - enables organisational learning and expedites the decision-making process (*faster* decision making)
  - promotes broader understanding and ownership of the organisation's strategic outlook, leading to enhanced execution and impact (*effective* decision making)
- integrated
  - drives strategic actions and innovation focus, enabling managers to *redefine* the organisation's strategic objectives (*cohesive* decision making)
- dynamic
  - enables ongoing *review* of management's strategic assumptions from a position of increased sensitivity to environmental signals (*earlier* decision making)
- repeatable
  - enables managers to *revise* strategic responses in line with emerging developments in the external operating environment.

This process is outlined in figure 4.3 (overleaf).

This approach to strategy design, with its emphasis on internal creativity, learning and collaboration, represents the company's investment in its strategic resource. In effect, it's an exercise in asset generation, beginning with one view of the world and the organisation's position within that world, and emerging with an original and differentiated strategic outlook that is a better *fit* for the future environment. Such a process respects the prioritisation that strategy deserves, and produces the distinct outlook that company boards and shareholders demand.

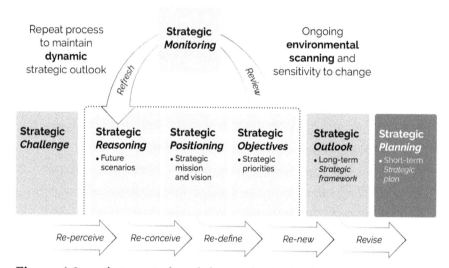

Figure 4.3: an integrated and dynamic strategic process

Such a process is an investment in the corporation's ultimate asset, its strategic outlook.

3. STRATEGY AS CREATIVITY

In March 2013 Domino's Pizza in Australia undertook a major media campaign raising awareness of an impending announcement that was set to be the 'biggest in 20 years'. 'You've DEMANDED CHANGE and we've pushed ourselves to RESPOND,' spruiked CEO Don Meij, the very public face of the campaign. Such was the weight of promotion that you couldn't help but be intrigued by the upcoming 'game changer' innovation. Would we soon be receiving drone-delivered pizzas? Would eating more pizzas be the key to future weight loss?

So what was all the fuss about? Why, the introduction of new topping choices and square pizza bases, of course.

The consumer ridicule was instant and the feedback was clear: 'What an underwhelming announcement!' But really, should we have been so surprised? While Domino's might provide a high-profile example, it's hardly an isolated case of incrementalism dressed up as innovation. The fact is most companies struggle with strategic and innovation creativity. And the major factor behind this struggle is thinking that remains 'anchored in the present'.[4]

Surrounded by the pervasive behaviours, policies and infrastructure of today, it's nigh impossible to imagine new ways of working that aren't 'anchored in the present'. And without breaking free from today's worldview, managers will always find it hard to innovate or to transform their business for the future in a timely manner.

Anchoring restricts the organisation to repeatedly producing incremental, 'faster horse' strategies[5], when a new type of thinking is required. We see examples of such incrementalism everywhere: doing things better within the current paradigm (cost cutting, outsourcing, shared services, reduced packaging sizes), rather than doing things differently to meet or establish a new paradigm. Overcoming strategic incrementalism therefore requires an escape from the overbearing context of the present. Scenarios hold the key to this perceptual freedom.

'Serengeti strategists': Scenarios are a powerful tool for breaking free from today's overbearing paradigms, which restrict managers to strategic incrementalism.

Reperceiving scenarios

To the uninitiated, scenarios can sometimes suffer from an image problem. They're associated with risk management or safety first, 'robust' strategies designed to work across multiple scenarios. In other words, they're seen as conservative, the Volvo of the planning world. And it's true, scenarios are incredibly useful for highlighting risk and understanding uncertainty. However, their greater value lies in uncovering strategic options and innovation opportunities.

I believe scenarios serve three purposes across what you might call a decision-making spectrum: a conservative purpose, a confirming purpose and a creative one. In turn, these deliver organisational benefits in the form of risk awareness, confidence to act and insight discovery (see figure 4.4).

The conservative purpose is served in terms of risk minimisation, identifying and understanding future uncertainty. This purpose tends to be protective, akin to the new coach of a losing sports team saying, 'Let's get our defence right before we start building our attack'.

But ultimately you need to score to win. And the other two purposes are far more attacking, more entrepreneurial. The first of these is confirming emerging thinking, providing the deeper understanding that supports previously held instincts and providing the catalyst that allows you to act with confidence.

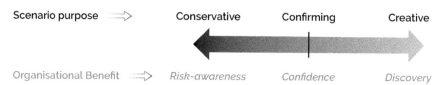

Figure 4.4: scenarios and the decision-making spectrum

Scenarios serve several purposes, delivering strategic benefits to the organisation in the form of risk awareness, confidence to act and discovery of fresh insights.

At a strategic planning workshop for an architectural design agency, scenarios were developed from which a strong theme of future suburban renewal emerged. In this scenario, local councils promoted policies to improve the proportion of residents who could work locally. As a result, community connection increased as people spent more time within their community and less time commuting to and from it. With reduced commuting, outer suburbs that were dominated by concrete and tarmac would begin to transition from a transportation culture to more of a village feel, with design placing greater emphasis on place and community interaction.

For the client, future opportunities in urban design were obvious. 'We need to increase our investment in this area. It's something we've discussed before but never felt compelled to act on.' The scenarios had confirmed their thinking. While the idea wasn't new, their clarity was. The scenarios had provided the impetus to act.

Transformational scenarios

Freed from the constrictions of the present, scenarios open up strategic thinking by providing different, future contexts from which the organisation can approach its strategic challenge. This different backdrop is the essential stimulus for unlocking creativity and discovering new insights. Mentally unshackled from 'what is', managers are able to hold up a mirror to their existing operations and competencies and assess strategic responses from a different perspective. This is the transformational impact of scenarios: helping the organisation to reperceive the future external environment, and using these fresh perceptions as the basis for reconceiving the organisation's identity, vision and objectives.

This transformational impact is what makes scenarios so powerful. Suddenly strategies that have been historically successful, or that continue to be successful in the present, are no longer assumed to be the eternal truths they were. More importantly, new strategies emerge that were previously blocked by the boundaries of today's paradigms. It's the different, future contexts, allowing managers to develop new worldviews, that present these opportunities in a new light.

Chapter 11 provides extensive coverage of a strategic planning project I facilitated during 2012–13 for the State Library of Victoria, 'What is a public library in 2030?' It's worth noting here the transformation in thinking that scenarios enabled over the course of this project. Before the development of two scenarios for 2030, and based on the interview responses from multiple industry stakeholders, my initial thinking was that one of the key issues for public libraries concerned the future of digital publishing rights, a perspective framed by the historical paradigm of libraries and books and the growing popularity of ebooks. This issue, while clearly important, represents classic incremental thinking.

The use of scenarios allowed new thinking to emerge that transcended the *libraries as books* paradigm. Suddenly, libraries could be legitimately conceived as creative hubs where content was generated as opposed to being managed and distributed, or as community hubs that facilitated active learning as opposed to passive content consumption. The issue of digital publishing rights consequently slipped down the order of importance as new, transformational strategic outlooks for public libraries emerged.

4. STRATEGY AS LEARNING

Strategic design is about organisational learning. This is hardly a new idea[6][7][8], but it was a concept I personally wrestled with for many years. Often during those times I was even dismissive of the idea, despite the fact that many of the scenario planners and strategists I most admired had written so enthusiastically on the topic.

During those years I was an unconscious subscriber to the *strategy as output* school of thought. To me, strategy was about doing, organisations were about getting things done, and learning was something you did on your own time.

When the penny finally dropped, it was a profound breakthrough for me. *Of course strategy is about learning!* It's the learning that enables original insights to surface. It's the learning that elevates strategy to a creative process.

The learning that occurs during the strategy process is in the form of a deeper understanding of the 'forces, relationships, and dynamics'[9] driving changes in the business environment, and their possible future impacts. This understanding provides the platform from which new thinking emerges. Without this learning, it's very hard to generate an original perception of the future and hence an original strategy.

And this is the struggle in which many businesses find themselves today, having adopted a disempowering approach to strategic design that essentially outsources the learning component of decision making. Overwhelmed by the almost unlimited availability of information, managers instead rely on forecasts that have been filtered by the judgement of others: consumer demand forecasts, market performance forecasts and so on. In effect, writes Peter Beck, former planning director of Shell UK, managers have abdicated their involvement in the decision-making process 'in favour of the experts'[10]: 'In what respect is he then a decision-maker?' he asks. 'In fact, the real decision-makers are the people … who sift available information, assess the … situation, and take decisions.'

The result of this abdication in favour of forecasts is a lack of organisational learning, which leads to a lack of strategic creativity, strategic originality and strategic fit.

Participatory strategic design enables learning because it requires managers to roll up their sleeves and get their hands dirty; to exercise their own judgement in exploring the forces shaping their business environment. The emphasis here is not on surface-level outcomes, but rather on the forces driving these outcomes. In turn, this hands-on approach is empowering in that it enables managers to develop their *own* feel for the future.

Acting with confidence

As for thousands of budding scenario planners, one of the first ports of call in my quest to better understand the method was *The Art of the Long View* by Peter Schwartz. This classic book had introduced scenarios to the masses since 1991 and appeared as a reference in most articles on scenario planning. So it was with great anticipation that I opened to the first page:

'This book is about freedom.'

Cue my disappointment and confusion. *Freedom? What an underwhelming opening,* I thought. *Scenarios aren't about freedom. They're about the future. What's that got to do with freedom?* It took me almost a decade to fully appreciate the wisdom of this opening line. Scenarios *are* about freedom. And the learning outcomes from creating scenarios provide this freedom.

Having explored the factors influencing their operating environment, how these factors might evolve and their possible future impacts, managers emerge from the scenario process with a broader and deeper understanding of the environment in which they have to function and compete. In turn, this learning provides a liberating dose of clarity:

- 'This is *what* we think could happen.'
- 'This is *why* we think it could happen.'
- 'This is *how* we think it could happen.'
- 'And this is *what* we intend to do about it.'

In this sense, the organisational learning that occurs is empowering. Scenarios *are* about freedom. They allow you to act with confidence on the original insights you generate. In turn, this confidence provides another nail in the coffin of the stereotype of scenarios as a conservative tool for risk management. According to Peter Beck, in practice the opposite actually tends to be true: 'The more the decision makers feel that they understand their environment, understand the dangers but also perceive potential opportunities, the more are they able to take riskier decisions.'[11]

Slowing down change

'Most managers are "energetic problem-solvers" busy working in the "here and now" trying to "solve problems",' suggests George Burt in an essay reviewing Pierre Wack's work. The problem, he argues, is: 'Few managers invest in learning about those systemic structures that are the root cause of such problems that is driving their actions'[12] (see figure 4.5).

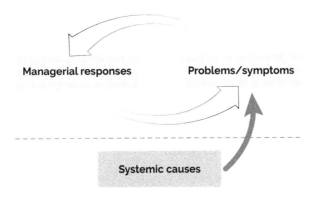

Managerial responses   **Problems/symptoms**

Systemic causes

Figure 4.5: strategy as output

In the absence of systemic understanding, organisations continue to be overwhelmed by problems in the 'here and now'.

The learning from scenarios 'slows down change'. Rather, change still occurs at the same pace; it's just not perceived to be disruptive or overwhelming, because the organisation is able to detect and make sense of it earlier and is rehearsed in its response. After all, it's not the rate of change itself but the lack of preparedness for change that constantly leaves managers feeling out of breath.

This effect of slowing down change can be likened to the different experiences of two drivers, an expert and a novice, approaching an intersection at 60 kilometres per hour. To the expert, the intersection approaches slowly; their perception of speed is moderated by a familiarity with the situation and their preparedness for what needs to be done. To the novice, on the other hand, the intersection approaches all too fast — the perceived suddenness of change stemming from a lack of preparation.

With an understanding of the underlying drivers of change and their possible outcomes, the organisation is vulnerable to fewer surprises from external developments. In effect, it moves from the defensive state of perpetual responsiveness to a proactive position of anticipation and confirmation.

Henceforth, surprises are subtracted from the future. You see headlines or issues or trends and you have an understanding of why they are occurring. While competitors continue to be caught unaware by unforeseen changes, you are seeing the unfolding of anticipated scenarios ('That makes sense'), providing the impression that the pace of change has indeed slowed down.

Making the future familiar

Of course, rehearsing the future is nothing new. Scenarios, simulation and visualisation have been commonplace for years in high-risk or high-performance fields where:

- the environment is uncertain (dynamic, complex, competitive)
- the stakes are high (military, firefighters, police, pilots, emergency services, astronauts, driving instructors)
- the performers are elite (athletes, artistic performers) (see figure 4.6).

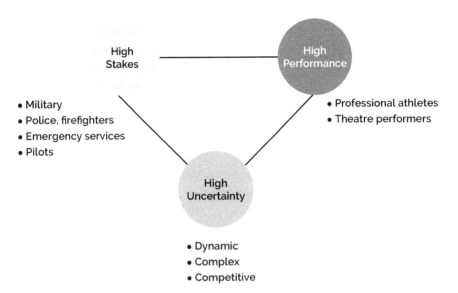

High Stakes — High Performance

- Military
- Police, firefighters
- Emergency services
- Pilots

- Professional athletes
- Theatre performers

High Uncertainty

- Dynamic
- Complex
- Competitive

Figure 4.6: who rehearses the future?

Elite operators in highly uncertain, high-stakes, high-performance industries recognise the benefits of rehearsing the future. So why not corporations?

The benefits of future rehearsal are undeniable in environments that are uncertain, involve high stakes or demand elite performance, where the aim is to make the future familiar. Of course, the military, the airline industry and professional sports are going to embrace scenarios, simulation and visualisation if they improve decision making and future performance. These operators are elite in their field and can't afford to leave any stone unturned in the pursuit of better results.

The characteristics of these future-rehearsing industries are not unique. Many can be applied equally to a competitive business environment. That the environment is uncertain is a given. The stakes are obviously high when decisions can have such an impact across people's livelihoods and communities. And most successful business managers would regard themselves as high performers. So why is it that the vast majority of organisations still prefer to 'play with reality itself'[13], rather than learning from the safe house of scenarios?

Slowing down change and the confidence that comes from making decisions in familiar situations are the business benefits from rehearsing the future. When significant changes do occur, you're not overwhelmed or rushed. You've been here before. You've rehearsed your responses and their possible consequences. And because of this experience, you make better decisions. You know what to do when early signals of change arise.

For the unprepared organisation, periods of significant transition are typically marked by confusion ('What's happening?'), uncertainty ('What should we do?') and reprisals ('Who's to blame?'). Caught by surprise, managers tend to react with hasty, inadequate responses that merely demonstrate their misreading of the situation, or else they are struck by strategic inertia, frozen by their inability to fully comprehend what is happening.

Consider the actions of US car executives in recent years. In the wake of the financial crisis in 2008, and with their iconic companies facing bankruptcy, they flew to Washington in their private jets to petition the government, cap in hand, to bail them out. Unsurprisingly, they were scorned for being 'out of touch' by the public and politicians alike. The next time these industry leaders made their way to the White House they arrived in eco-friendly vehicles, belatedly determined to demonstrate that their companies were moving with the times.

Or the Victorian taxi industry, which I discuss further in chapter 6. Rocked by the unforeseen emergence of Uber as a competitor, and perhaps unaware of the dearth of community goodwill, the industry decided to get on the front foot via a Twitter campaign. In an attempt to bolster their position in the minds of the community, and in a clear case of overreach, they launched a hashtag campaign called #YourTaxis, inviting the public to share their positive taxi experiences on social media. You can guess how that ended. After only a couple of hours, the campaign had to be shut down and the industry was no longer in any doubt about their customers' dissatisfaction.

What these examples demonstrate is that when confronted with unexpected circumstances, and in the absence of any future rehearsal, often the best you can hope for is to scramble your way forward. On the other hand, for the prepared organisation, discontinuities provide an opportunity for purposeful growth and a rapid gain in market share.

Note: The significant strategic benefit of slowing down change is covered further in chapter 13.

5. STRATEGY AS PARTICIPATION

In an oft-quoted 1982 article in *Fortune* magazine titled 'Corporate Strategists Under Fire', Walter Kiechel III declared, '90% of organizations fail to execute on strategy effectively'.[14] The authority of this relatively high failure figure has been debated ever since. Another feature on why business leaders fail, published almost 20 years later, estimated that in 70 per cent of cases the failure of CEOs could be put down to poor strategy execution.[15]

Whether 50, 70 or 90 per cent of strategies are poorly executed is beside the point. The fact is the figure remains too high and companies continue to be notoriously poor at implementing their plans. This poor conversion rate is strategy's albatross, and I was reminded of this burden when preparing for a workshop for a large regional council: 'Be aware', I was informed, 'that the CEO thinks most strategies are nothing more than a marketing exercise and that 9 out of 10 corporate plans are rubbish.'

So why does successful strategy execution remain such a problem?

Perhaps the answer lies in how we define and subsequently treat strategy. When we think of strategy we tend to think of the act of strategic design, the formulation component of the process. Execution of this strategy is thought of as a separate activity undertaken by a different set of individuals. In other words, the two activities are treated as distinct—*the thinkers do the thinking, the doers do the doing, and never the twain shall meet* (see figure 4.7).

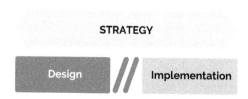

Figure 4.7: the separation of strategic design and implementation

Businesses have traditionally treated the activities of strategic design and strategy implementation as distinct, which has contributed to poor execution effectiveness.

The result of this 'artificial separation'[16] is a lack of:

- organisational understanding of the logic that underpins the strategy
- institutional belief in the strategy
- ownership of the strategy
- effective implementation.

Removing this schism, it would seem, is central to improving strategy execution.

Why can't the 'doers' be involved in the strategy design? Is there the implicit assumption that the implementers 'aren't smart enough' or 'don't know enough', and therefore any resultant strategy would be 'dumbed down'? This view was made apparent to me when I was working with a CEO and one of his general managers in putting together a list of employees to take part in an upcoming scenario planning project. When the name of one employee was mentioned, the CEO briefly considered their involvement before shooting it down with the statement, 'He's not really strategic'. How condescending, I thought. As organisational learning pioneer Arie de Geus has said,

'Brilliance is not a monopoly of a company's top levels, neither is producing solutions the prerogative of specialists.'[17]

Perhaps for too long, too much emphasis has been placed on the *primary* design component of strategy, to the detriment of the *secondary*, equally important component, execution. After all, excellent design cannot overcome poor execution, and neither can excellent execution make up for any shortfalls in design. Strategic success requires that design and implementation be treated as equal and integrated components of strategy (see figure 4.8). And this means bringing the 'thinkers' and 'doers' together during the design stage.

STRATEGY

Design   Implementation

Figure 4.8: a participatory strategy process

Strategic success depends on the integration of strategy design and implementation; they are not mutually exclusive.

Participatory learning

When strategic design and implementation are treated as distinct, communication of the strategy to the broader organisation tends to follow a familiar pattern: a briefing session is scheduled where those next in line down the hierarchy are informed of the new strategy; in a corporate form of Chinese whispers, attendees (the 'chief implementers') are then expected to brief their staff, and so on.

In many instances, these meetings might condense months or even years of research, modelling and iterative conversations into a one-hour PowerPoint presentation. To expect that the audience, those responsible for putting this theory into practice, will be able or willing to grasp, remember or buy into the complexities, logics, implications and opportunities inherent in these presentations is a big ask. And yet this is exactly what is expected: 'We've done our job—now it's up to you.'

If company-wide strategic understanding, belief and ownership are so low, is it any wonder that strategic implementation is poor? In fact, while individuals vary in their 'learning styles', it is generally agreed that passive learning methods such as lecture-style formats are among the least effective modes from which people learn, and that more interactive methods such as group discussions or simulation (learning by doing) lead to higher learning and retention rates. And this makes intuitive sense; the more involved learners are in the activity the more likely they will be to remember and utilise the materials they have learned.

Translate this theory to improving strategy processes within a company. Rather than being recipients of the completed strategy product, the 'implementers' would be active participants in its formulation. They would be involved in the conversations about external forces influencing their industry's future. They would discuss the possible implications these forces represent to their company, and they would consider the organisation's response. It's from these conversations that shared learning, and a shared language, emerges.

For the organisation, the result of such collaborative strategic design is a far broader base of understanding of the company's strategic reasoning ('I understand why we're doing what we're doing'). From this understanding springs belief ('I have confidence in what we're doing') and ownership ('I am committed to what we're doing because I was involved in its development'). Understanding, belief and ownership are the keys to improved execution (see figure 4.9). And as others 'down the line' are updated, it's from a position of first-hand knowledge and passion—the corporate strategy now has an army of internal advocates.

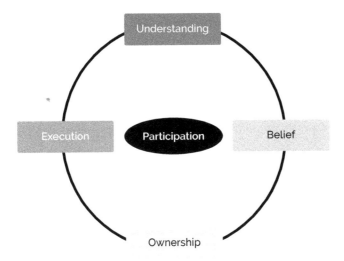

Figure 4.9: strategic momentum

Participatory strategic design mobilises the organisation's intellectual resources, along with its energy and passion.

Speeding up decision making

Arie de Geus categorises corporate decisions as either routine or non-routine. Routine decisions are those for which management and employees already have the necessary knowledge and experience that allow them to respond effectively. These decisions can usually be made quickly and fairly instinctively. Non-routine decisions, on the other hand, tend to be larger in scale, often requiring major internal changes in response to external change. These decisions are far less common and far more important, as they define a company's future direction at critical junctures.

Non-routine decisions also tend to take 'an inordinate amount of time to be implemented', especially when treated as the domain of an exclusive club:

> **We found that decisions taken by isolated small groups [external consultants] producing a brilliant idea always seemed to run into difficulties when it came to implementation - the rest of the company did not want to do it or did not understand it...**

> **Therefore, it seemed important that the implementers are part of the learning and decision-making process, otherwise an awful lot of time is wasted in the implementation phase.[20]**

In other words, participatory strategy development speeds up non-routine decision-making.

In his book *The Living Company*, de Geus describes the four typical stages of the decision-making process as perceiving, embedding, concluding and acting[21]:

1. **Perceiving.** An issue is detected that requires attention and action.
2. **Embedding.** Efforts are made to learn about and understand the issue.
3. **Concluding.** Decisions are rehearsed regarding the organisation's response to the issue.
4. **Acting.** The organisation implements its response to the issue.

Expressed linearly against time (t0–t4), these four phases appear, with the aforementioned breakdown in implementation indicated, in figure 4.10.

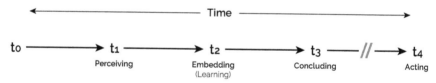

Figure 4.10: de Geus's four phases of decision making

Driven by a belief that the critical success factor in any decision-making process is speed measured between perceiving and action (t1 → t4), de Geus helped to instigate the use of collaborative 'play' in decision making, allowing managers to experiment using simulation and scenarios. Not only did the rate of institutional learning accelerate (another critical success factor!), but so too did the speed of decision making. In fact, for non-routine decisions, the introduction of a collaborative approach to experiential learning through the use of scenarios improved the speed of decisions by a factor of 2. Necessary, fundamental changes to the business were now being implemented at twice their former speed[22] (see figure 4.11).

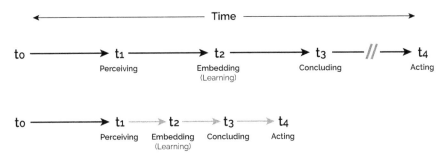

Figure 4.11: accelerating decision making

Participatory scenario development, with its emphasis on organisational learning, can halve the time between perceiving and acting on strategic issues.

Yet even this significant improvement doesn't fully capture the benefits derived from collaborative strategy development. While de Geus emphasises the improved speed between organisational perceiving and acting (t1 → t4), further improvement still lies in the initial act of perceiving (t0 → t1) (see figure 4.12).

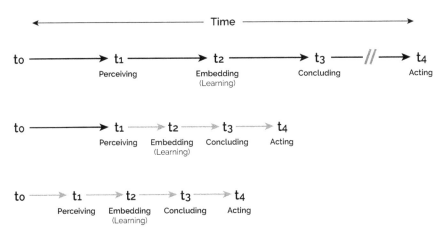

Figure 4.12: earlier decision making

The priming effect of scenarios improves managerial sensitivity to external change, further accelerating the decision-making process.

Emerging from the scenario process with an enhanced understanding of industry dynamics and possible future outcomes, the organisation now has a framework for anticipating external changes. Such a framework enables it to perceive changes or issues of significance earlier, thereby reducing the perception gap (t0 ➜ t1). This is the priming effect of scenarios.

Note: The significant benefit of increased organisational sensitivity to early signals of change is covered extensively in chapter 13.

CHAPTER 5

Overcoming myopia

Strategy requires a broad contextual outlook

In 2004 a story in *The Roanoke Times* led with a photograph of an obviously pregnant woman standing outside her home smoking a cigarette.[1] The story reported on complaints about a noisy road construction project that had been disrupting local traffic. The photo caption noted the woman's concern about the effect of exposing her unborn child to the sound of jackhammers. The story remained a local issue. The photo went viral around the world.

And so it is for organisations; myopia causes us to miss vital signals that are sometimes literally under our noses. While attention tends to focus on the obvious, the 'noisiest', the here and now, at the same time, less obvious changes holding future significance tend to pass unnoticed until it's too late. And why is this? Because passion is a vortex.

Senior managers are passionate people who become absorbed in their job. They get up at 5 am to send and reply to emails. They arrive at work early and are often among the last to leave. They make and take business calls late at night, on their holidays and at weekends.

And they socialise with colleagues into the evening, taking every opportunity to talk all things 'work'. This passion and hard work underpins their career success. It's what they're admired for by their peers, and they wear it as a badge of honour. *Yet passion is the foundation of industry myopia.*

Managers are also industry experts. It's this expertise that allows them to make routine decisions instinctively and to speak with authority about their industry. As their experience builds, they develop paradigm attachment, becoming more and more wedded to the way things are, to the things they know, and dismissing with authority (*certainty*) any new ideas that aren't their own—'I know how this industry works... that'll never happen!' They begin to believe their industry is unique and that only they, with their superior knowledge, have the strategic answers. As the Zen teacher Shunryu Suzuki expressed it, 'In the beginner's mind there are many possibilities, but in the expert's there are few.'[2] *Expertise builds industry myopia.*

Managers have access to industry data—lots and lots of industry data. It's their security blanket. They rely on this information to make *fact-based* decisions, to back their 'gut feel' judgements and to respond to market share emergencies. They take pride in knowing this data, and in drawing on it publicly to reinforce perceptions of knowledge and authority. *Data reinforces industry myopia.*

Managerial passion, expertise and data combine to produce a myopia vortex at the top that seeps down through the organisation (see figure 5.1). And industry myopia is the primary reason change is experienced as disruption—'We didn't see that coming!'

Myopic mayhem

During the first eight years of my time at Foster's, on the first business day of each month senior executives lived for the release of the previous month's market share figures. These figures were rarely available before 2 pm, yet without fail the CEO would phone through an enquiry at 11 am. At midday the marketing director would do a casual walk-by 'just to see if they had arrived'. By 1 pm the marketing vice president, a highly strung man at the best of times, would make his anxiety felt. Each of them was beyond eager to get their hands on the unofficial industry scorecard that would affirm or disconfirm our most recent performance. Either we were on track or we weren't.

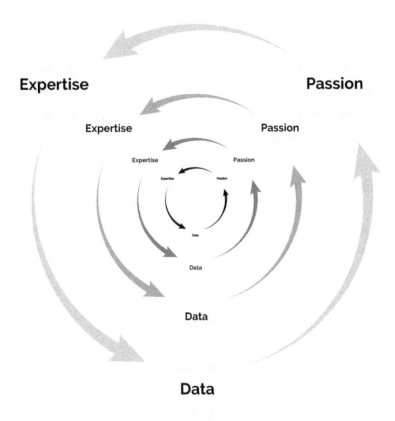

Figure 5.1: a myopia vortex

Passion, expertise and data combine to narrow the organisation's focus on its immediate industry, while impairing its perception of future impending shifts.

As a young market researcher tasked with delivering these results to senior executives, I felt like I was on the set of *Charlie and the Chocolate Factory*, for I had the golden ticket (hand delivery only, of course — it was much too important to email).

Then would come the reaction. If the results were positive, the office mood would lighten instantly. Everyone was doing a good job ('Keep up the great work'). If the results were poor, however, those in the know would speak in hushed tones and the finger-pointing would begin ('What do you people do around here anyway?').

And then the response. If results were disappointing it was usually predictable. Invitation-only meetings in the 'War Room' (clichéd, but true). Discounts on key brands, more aggressive promotions, focus groups to find out what consumers were thinking, or perhaps some new packaging or advertising was needed? Invariably the results would then reverse the following month, in which case it was our competitors' turn to respond. And so the manic short-term cycle would continue.

Eventually the decision was made to drop this monthly report. Living tactically from one month to the next had gotten out of hand. It was as though the company's psyche revolved around our monthly results and the activities of our competitors. A circuit-breaker was needed. It was a far-sighted and brave call that not everyone agreed with ('How will we know who's winning if we don't keep score?'). Yet the sky didn't fall in, as the sceptics might have expected. In fact, the opposite was true. Almost immediately our focus switched to playing a longer game and the market share bible that had driven the bipolar behaviour of competing corporate giants was instantly forgotten. It was barely mentioned again.

This example of industry myopia and the behaviour it promotes is hardly unique; it's repeated interminably around the world. Like a young child in a foot race, companies head towards the future with their focus firmly on their competitors. At Foster's we even formalised this myopic outlook by creating the position of *Competitor Analyst*; a role with the specific task of reporting on the activities of our major beer rival.

Such an insular focus narrows the organisation's sense of identity. It comes to define itself by what it does and in relation to what its most obvious competitors are doing. And when managers finally look up, they find that the world has shifted and that the assumptions upon which they've based their decisions are no longer valid. In effect, myopia causes managers to see the current state of their industry *too well*. At the same time, significant changes outside their immediate proximity appear a little fuzzy or go unnoticed, or are simply ignored — until it's too late.

As Peter Senge noted in his book *The Fifth Discipline*, close-knit industries can be especially vulnerable to strategic surprise 'because all the member companies look to each other for standards of best practice'.[3] So rather than being a signal of future certainty, similarity of industry practice can point to a lack of certainty, as competing companies, united in their uncertainty about the future, settle for a sort of 'false consensus'.[4] This is the danger of industry benchmarking.

Context is everything

Overcoming myopia begins with situating the organisation and its transactional environment within the broader context of society.[5] Such a perspective recognises the deeper causal relationships that enable and drive industry dynamics and outcomes. Understanding what these causal relationships are, how they might change and how they could affect future operating dynamics is the essence of scenario planning.

The transactional environment is the arena in which the organisation participates, where the perceived value or benefits it creates are exchanged to satisfy perceived wants and needs. The organisation has an immediate relationship with this environment. The actions of industry stakeholders can have a direct influence on the organisation; and through its policies and actions, the organisation can exert direct influence on industry outcomes. Actors within this environment include customers, employees, distributors, suppliers, regulators, competitors, unions and other relevant participants (see figure 5.2, overleaf).

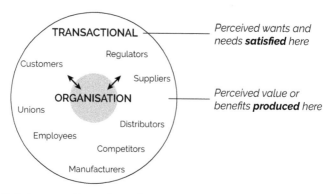

Figure 5.2: transactional environment

The attention-consuming transactional environment is merely a subset of broader society.

The dynamics of the transactional environment are invariably enabled or driven by factors beyond the industry's boundaries. Within this broader social environment are the deeper, less obvious factors influencing industry dynamics, including demographics, social values, technology, climate, legislation, employment levels and interest rates.

Together these factors evolve, interact and combine to provide a shifting and dynamic context for the organisation's operations. At any given time, a unique mix of factors is interacting to produce a particular operating context. And as changes occur across each of these factors, this mix changes, shaping the attitudes, behaviours, wants and needs of society, and ultimately influencing the benefits customers seek from your business (see figure 5.3).

This shifting contextual dynamic serves up a series of ongoing *strategic fitness* tests where the corporate challenge is to remain in alignment with the environment. Such volatility highlights the folly of strategic inertia or, worse, managerial hubris, a point well made by Theodore Levitt in his classic article 'Marketing Myopia'.[6] 'In truth, there is no such thing as a growth industry,' he argued. 'There are only companies organized and operated to create and capitalize on growth opportunities. Industries that assume themselves to be riding some automatic growth escalator invariably descend into stagnation.'

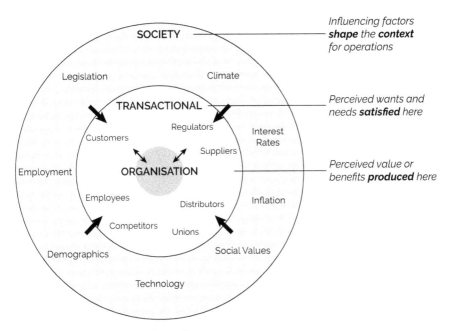

Figure 5.3: contextual environment

The changing social context serves up a series of ongoing strategic fitness tests that challenge the organisation to remain in alignment with its environment.

Note: The topic of identifying strategically significant causal relationships is covered extensively in chapter 9.

By instead adopting a contextual outlook, historical trends, and the forecasts based on these trends, are put into perspective. You are able to look at your historical performance, not from the position of absolute outcomes and trends, but from the deeper perspective of underlying drivers and conditions that led to those outcomes. The result is an appreciation for society's fluency and a broader outlook towards the future.

CHAPTER 6

The shape of things to come

It is possible to anticipate embryonic issues and opportunities before they emerge

In 2011 the Victorian State Government announced a major inquiry into the taxi industry, to be chaired by Professor Allan Fels. The inquiry investigated all aspects of the industry and recommended a set of reforms focusing on achieving better outcomes for the public.

The subsequent report, released in November 2012, has come under criticism because not once in its 240 pages is the word *Uber* mentioned, yet within three years Uber would seem to be the only word on the minds of all those involved with the industry. The easy assessment was that the report was worthless because it didn't warn the industry of its imminent disruption.

I hold a different view. In fact, on page one Professor Fels is explicit in his warnings about the future of the industry. So, for those of you who don't have the time to digest all 240 pages, let me save you the effort by directing your attention to the foreword:

The inquiry could have gone much further in its approach to removing restrictions on taxi and hire car licences. In effect,

Victoria's taxi industry has operated for years as a 'closed shop', with a small number of licence holders protected from the effects of competition at the expense of consumers, taxi operators and drivers (who continue to experience low remuneration, poor work conditions and a risky work environment). The inquiry found no public interest for allowing this situation to continue.

Professor Fels' frustration with the industry's efforts to defy reform are clear:

The industry must bear considerable responsibility for its efforts to prevent past governments from adopting fundamental reform and for failing to take action to lift performance, increase service availability and attract and retain quality drivers. Now, with high levels of customer dissatisfaction and low occupancy rates threatening the industry's future, these elements should not be allowed to derail essential reforms.

In other words, PEOPLE DON'T LIKE YOU AND YOU ARE RIPE FOR DISRUPTION! Poor levels of customer service over a sustained period had drained the industry of customer goodwill. The industry was tolerated, but not liked. Customer usage was not due to any sense of loyalty, but rather to a lack of choice. Yet, seemingly immune from the effects of competition, the industry felt no compulsion to improve services — until the illusion of regulatory protection was usurped by a combination of technology and changing social values.

In effect, the taxi industry disrupted itself! The disruption was due to the industry's inadequate response to an obvious embryonic issue: the unresolved tension that customers felt with regard to poor customer service.

Rarely easy to detect, the ability to anticipate and prepare for the emergence of strategically significant embryonic issues and opportunities *before* they develop is perhaps the greatest planning skill an organisation can have.

Understanding change

The progress of change through society, whether it be beliefs, issues, systems or behaviours, tends to follow the shape of a bell curve.[1][2][3] This curve shows social change moving through four distinct stages: an *embryonic* phase, an *emerging* phase, an *established* phase and an *eroding* phase (see figure 6.1). As change passes through this cycle, existing social behaviours change as new paradigms emerge to become established over time.

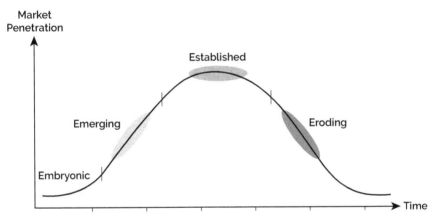

Figure 6.1: social change tends to follow the shape of a bell curve
Eventually the idea whose time has come becomes an idea whose time has passed.

During the *embryonic* phase, future issues or trends appear as weak signals and lack statistical significance. This early stage of development is a hotbed of future change, where today's unmet needs, dirty secrets, cultural hypocrisies, unresolved tensions, systemic inequities and slow-burning issues lie in wait as silent epidemics, before emerging as tomorrow's headline acts.

Importantly, this emergence is event-dependent, rather than time-dependent. Because the issue already exists, it is like dry tinder: it only needs a spark, an enabler, an event, to quickly emerge and grow. This is why embryonic issues can seemingly emerge overnight and why they are so significant.

The *emerging* phase of social change marks the period of exponential growth. This is the phase of rapid adoption, when new behaviour is typically referred to as a trend. During this stage, established protocols are challenged and companies are forced to adapt their products and services in line with new expectations to maintain relevance. Those companies that didn't foresee the shift are relegated to the role of *market follower* and usually enter a sustained period of *me-too* innovation.

Until this acceleration occurs, embryonic signals are often disregarded as being random, disconnected or fringe, and are easily dismissed because of history or a lack of evidence ('That'll never happen').

After the acceleration occurs, well … 'Who would have thought … ?'[4]

As it matures, the emerging trend becomes *established* behaviour, a new social norm. The once exciting trend comes to represent mainstream activity. It is reduced to being merely average — average working hours, average household expenditure, average age at marriage and so on. In fact, once established, a trend that had been seen as a novelty comes to be taken for granted ('That's just the way we do things around here'). Our senses are dulled by its ubiquity (*paradigm blindness*). The only mystery remaining is how long it will prevail before its replacement by the next embryonic upstart!

Over time the established behaviour begins to decline: when previous problems are resolved, it becomes *redundant*; when superior solutions emerge, it is *usurped*; when its 'false' part is revealed, it becomes *problematic*. Just as every paradigm provides solutions, it also creates problems. Eventually each system reaches its limits: unintended consequences emerge, problems develop, these problems reach a tipping point and a new paradigm, a new way of thinking and acting, emerges.[5] Thus, having effectively served its purpose, the cycle of change enters its *eroding* phase as new solutions are sought, new technologies arrive, and new ideas and behaviours develop.

Anticipating embryonic issues and opportunities

When we asked the question at Foster's, 'How do we get ahead of trends?', what we were really asking was, 'How do we get better at anticipating embryonic issues and opportunities *before* they emerge?'

If emerging trends are always preceded by a tail of weaker signals, then disruptive change is due not so much to the absence of signals, as it is to do with organisations having either (i) poor detection (failure to look in the right spots) or (ii) poor perception (failure to attach relevance to the signals).

Because embryonic issues appear as weak signals lacking statistical significance, the usual supporting mechanism of data is not available. Understanding processes for change is much more important. Over the years I've come to rely on seven techniques for identifying and anticipating the emergence of embryonic issues and opportunities:

1. dirty secrets
2. cultural hypocrisies
3. unresolved tensions
4. systemic inequities
5. slow-burning issues
6. social values
7. scenarios.

These techniques deliver organisational benefits across internal and external issues management and opportunity identification domains. Of course, the applications and benefits from these techniques are not entirely discrete. Some are effective across multiple domains—particularly unresolved tensions (are you the cause of the issue or the potential resolution?) and scenarios (which enable you to reframe how you see the external environment and how you view your internal operations). Represented graphically, the applications and benefits of these techniques are mapped in figure 6.2 (overleaf).

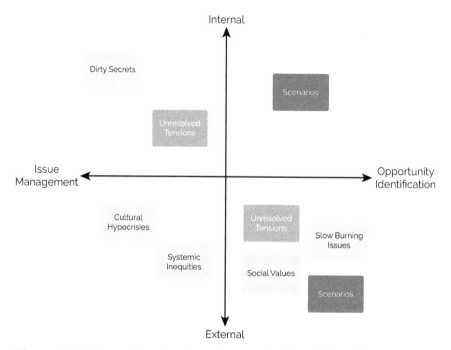

Figure 6.2: internal and external organisational benefits

Techniques for identifying and anticipating embryonic issues and opportunities deliver organisational benefits across multiple domains.

Let me explain what I mean by each of these techniques.

1. Dirty secrets

When looking for sources of future change, the natural inclination is to look externally, to what is happening *out there*. However, dirty secrets are about what's happening *in here*, uncovering the organisation's enemies within that have the capacity to cause self-implosion. In my experience, most organisations and industries have their share of dirty secrets. And almost without exception, managers are very poor at addressing these issues *ahead* of a crisis.

While we remain fascinated by the potential for external discontinuities, recent events have demonstrated the disruptive capacity of internal dirty secrets when they are exposed. In chapter 1,

I describe how the images of mistreated cattle in Indonesia brought Australia's live beef export industry to its knees. Not to be outdone, and showing they had learned nothing from this episode, four years later the Australian greyhound racing industry found itself facing a similar public backlash. This time it was the industry secret of live baiting that was exposed to an unknowing public. Live baiting refers to the illegal practice of using live animals (rabbits, piglets or possums) in the training of greyhounds. Once again, an appalled public demanded action, threatening the industry's existence and moving the NSW premier to announce his intention to close the industry down. Politics determined that the premier ultimately did not get his wish, though significant and lasting damage was done to the industry's image and reputation.

CONFRONTING DIRTY SECRETS

Since their preservation relies on public ignorance, transparency is the enemy of dirty secrets. To confront these internal issues, managers, industry leaders and governments need to ask themselves:

Which practices are the public unaware of, but if they were, it would alter their perception of who *we are and what we do?*

Addressing these practices before they are inevitably exposed provides an opportunity to tackle your organisation's soft underbelly or areas of vulnerability. In the age of transparency you have to accept that eventually these issues will be exposed. This inevitability presents managers with two innovation pathways:

- **offensive innovation**. This is the easy road. Proactively addressing the issue allows you to remain in control of your own destiny. Such action can also enable you to outmanoeuvre competitors with similar practices, who will be forced to defend their positions or to follow your lead.

- **defensive innovation**. This is the hard road. In responding to a public outcry, regulatory enforcement or the strategic moves of competitors, you are in effect shutting the gate after the horse has bolted. Such reaction ensures you lose control of the public narrative and outsource your destiny to the media, the public and legislators.

From the outside at least, choosing the offensive route appears to be in the best long-term interests of the organisation. Yet, with their mindset and behaviours conditioned by a pre-transparency era, managers invariably choose to play a form of Russian roulette with their organisation's future.

The truth is, while the earlier question is relatively easy to ask, managers find it hard to answer. It requires a high level of honest introspection and courage to confront what are effectively inconvenient truths, and the incentives to do so aren't necessarily great, given that organisational heretics are rarely rewarded with instant gratitude. So instead of action, you tend to hear denials and excuses:

'This is what we've always done.'

'Everyone else is doing it.'

'This is how we make a dollar.'

'What the public don't know won't hurt them, right?'

In the age of transparency, this last evasion is particularly misguided.

But in their defence, even brutal honesty and courage may not always be enough to identify internal dirty secrets. Often managers simply can't see the silent epidemics right under their noses. And the reason for this is that they suffer from *paradigm blindness*.

2. Cultural hypocrisies

As every good magician knows, context is the key to an effective illusion. Our judgements and decisions are inevitably influenced by the environment in which we make them. It's the same with cultural hypocrisies. Behaviours that are accepted in one context are considered unacceptable in another.

Cultural hypocrisies are enabled by the paradigm blindness that results from sustained exposure to a certain set of conditions (in our workplace, community or country, for example). Over time the prevalent conditions and understandings shape our perceptions and behaviours until we subconsciously adopt them as the way things are — we become blind to the paradigm in which we exist.

Our perception is heavily influenced by the social, cultural or organisational context in which we have been indoctrinated. As a result, we can be blind to inconsistencies, injustices and hypocrisies that may appear obvious to an outsider. Context familiarity thus conceals the embryonic issue.

Sledging in sport is the act of 'verballing' an opponent to gain an advantage. It's a behaviour practised and accepted in many sports, justified by a win-at-all-costs mentality and the old-school motto that 'what happens on the field stays on the field'. No international sporting team is more notorious for sledging than the Australian cricket team. Famously promoted by former Australian captain Steve Waugh as a legitimate tactic to bring about their opponents' 'mental disintegration', sledging was tolerated by an Australian public who expected their national team to play a tough, uncompromising, 'in your face' style of cricket.

Yet such behaviour is not tolerated in other spheres of life, or indeed in most other sports. And herein lies the blinding influence of paradigms. What would be seen elsewhere as poor sportsmanship is celebrated as 'part of the game' in cricket. Yet where does this appear in the rule book? What if this behaviour occurred in another context? Imagine how the public would react to the following story:

Rafael Nadal and Roger Federer are locked in a thrilling final at Wimbledon. It's 5-all in the fifth set and Nadal is serving. A 20-shot rally ends with a passing shot down the line that eludes the diving Federer. Instead of returning to the service line,

Nadal continues to stare down his opponent, spits on the ground in Federer's direction and calls him a 'weak so-and-so' for missing the shot. The royal box is not amused.

Recognising cultural hypocrisies is important for two reasons:

1. It's society's paradigm blindness that gives many organisations and industries the 'social licence' to operate as they do. This ongoing permission is therefore particularly fragile, relying as it does on the ongoing acceptance of an *inconsistent* point of view by the broader community.

2. Given the right events or change in circumstances, cultural hypocrisies are ripe for rapid or disruptive change.

EXPOSING CULTURAL HYPOCRISIES

Events that make us stop and think, waking us from our paradigm blindness, are the key to exposing cultural hypocrisies. Febfast, a month-long alcohol-free initiative aimed at raising awareness and redefining Australia's drinking culture, is one such event. Buy Nothing New, an annual campaign to raise awareness of our embedded consumption culture, is another.

In particular, extreme or exceptional events shake our existing perceptions and give impetus to the rise of new perceptions because they reframe the way we see issues: while the issue may not be new, our perception of it is ('I had no idea this was going on ... we need to do something about this').

In March 2018 the Australian cricket team became embroiled in a ball-tampering incident that made headlines around the world. Angered by their team's willingness to cheat, the public demanded severe penalties. As a result, three players were suspended, including the captain and vice-captain, and the coach resigned. This extreme event shone a light on the broader cultural and behavioural decay of the team, and the corrosive impact of a win-at-all-costs mentality. The scandal was described as a watershed moment in Australian cricket. Former coach John Buchanan, for example, commented, 'There's a feeling in Australia this isn't just a one-off incident. It's been building over a long period of time and the culture between the team needs to be addressed really seriously.'[6] In the public backlash, the act of sledging was effectively recast as the unsportsmanlike behaviour it had always been.

This illustration is typical of organisations that don't acknowledge the fragile foundations of their operations and that push the barrow too far, in the process putting their entire industry at risk. Consider paparazzi photographers and the tabloid magazines that profit from their intrusive exploits. This industry is essentially in the business of stalking famous individuals, employing practices that would be deemed illegal in other contexts but are permitted on the basis that somehow 'celebrities are different'—an incredibly weak premise on which to base an entire industry's profits. The last thing tabloids should be doing is publishing topless photos of British royals that only serve to shock the public from their paradigm blindness.

Foresightful organisations, on the other hand, are aware of the cultural hypocrisies or fragile perceptions that shore up their operations, are alert to the events that might cause these perceptions to change, and take action to prevent such events from occurring. In other words, *they don't poke the sleeping bear.*

Considerations for the anticipatory organisation include:

- What cultural hypocrisies underpin our operations or performance?
- What events might cause the public to overcome their paradigm blindness with regard to these hypocrisies?
- How can we manage our operations to prevent these events from occurring?

3. Unresolved tensions

As illustrated in the taxi industry example at the start of this chapter, unresolved tensions exist where people tolerate an issue but they don't like it. In the absence of viable alternatives, the lack of agency often results in a sort of resigned public acceptance ('What can you do?'). The frustration experienced daily by commuters battling traffic congestion on their way to work provides a contemporary example of an unresolved tension. Another is the popular dissatisfaction with politicians and the political system that has exploded so spectacularly across the globe in recent years, yet like most unresolved tensions this political backlash was predictable to anyone paying attention to the right signals.[7]

Ask yourself, how many people would respond positively to the following questions?

- Do you trust your politicians?
- Do you think politicians spend your tax money wisely?

The overwhelmingly negative responses to these questions point to why the popularity of the 'outsiders' Donald Trump and Bernie Sanders during the 2016 US primary elections should have come as no surprise. The political system was ripe for disruption. This example is discussed further in chapter 13.

With unresolved tensions, it's the unmet desire for a better way that leads to rapid adoption and change when a seemingly superior alternative finally presents itself. To use another political example, on the evening of 23 June 2010, Australians went to bed with one prime minister and woke up the next day with another. Overnight a challenge had taken place in which the leader of the country, Kevin Rudd, was deposed by his deputy, Julia Gillard. The swiftness of the coup caught everyone by surprise. Everyone, that is, except Rudd's political party colleagues.

Kevin Rudd had swept to power in November 2007 and enjoyed near-record public approval for the following two years. Out of the public eye, however, this esteem was not shared by his colleagues, many of whom despised him. For Rudd, his public support was the safety net that ensured his party's tolerance. When this support dropped significantly in the early months of 2010, Rudd's security blanket vanished. Such was his unpopularity with his colleagues that he didn't even bother contesting the leadership ballot in June 2010. An opening presented itself and the prime minister's colleagues acted. The immediate tensions were resolved.

IDENTIFYING UNRESOLVED TENSIONS

Disruption is the most overused term in business today. It is often used by managers under stress as a sort of 'get out of jail' free card. Too often they point to the effects of technology and complain, 'We were disrupted', as if some unavoidable act of god had taken away their company's natural right to prosperity. This is a cop-out, a way of deflecting the blame away from their own lack of effective internal processes, which should have enabled them to anticipate impending change.

Most so-called disruption is self-inflicted. Technology has democratised choice and the capacity to act (agency); more individuals and more companies are now capable of delivering customer solutions. Technology is not the disruptor, however; it is merely a facilitator to a different way of operating. Whether the new or different way of operating is 'better' is for the industry incumbents to decide. It's the opportunity for improvement (of services, for example) that provides the gateway for disruption.

In 2016 I stayed overnight in a five-star hotel in the centre of Adelaide. You know when you stay in these hotels that once you enter the building you're going to be robbed blind. This is especially so when you order room service ('A toasted sandwich sir? Certainly—that'll be $25'), but hey, *what can you do?* Even with these low expectations, however, I was shocked when checking out the next day to see that my bill for room service included an additional $6 delivery fee (a fee flagged in the tiniest of print—which of course no one reads—on page one of the in-room dining menu).

To me, this was just another example of an industry driving its own demise. If you're going to sneakily charge people extra for delivery on top of what are already exorbitant prices, then don't cry foul when you start losing customers to alternatives like Airbnb. And don't ask me if I want to join your mailing list!

In the age of agency democratisation, customer goodwill (an outcome of quality service) is priceless, and companies should never mistake usage for loyalty. More than ever, the question to ask is, 'Do we give our customers a reason to stay?'

ADDRESSING UNRESOLVED TENSIONS

Unresolved tensions are rarely hidden or unknown. Identifying them is not the problem; solving them is. Having said that, often it's not until a solution to the existing problem arrives, or an opening to a better way presents itself, that the actual scale of resentment becomes clear.

Unresolved tensions can be both an internal issue and an external opportunity. At an organisational level, managers need to confront the irritations they cause their customers, because if you don't fix them someone else will:

- What are the frustrations customers have with our products or services?
- What roadblocks do our processes or regulations put in the way of the customer's experience?
- What unnecessary margins can others target?
- Do we give our customers a reason to stay?

At a broader societal level, unresolved tensions represent opportunities for the anticipatory organisation:

- Which issues are tolerated that are universally disliked or drive people to despair?
- Which issues have the potential to emerge as unresolved tensions in the future?

4. Systemic inequities

After leaving Shell in the early 1980s, Pierre Wack began consulting for South African mining giant Anglo American. At the time South Africa was the lowest-cost producer of gold, an outcome made possible by its apartheid policies. Wack warned his client that their good fortune was coming to an end. South Africans imagined they were 'blessed with a geological miracle: their gold and diamond deposits', he argued perceptively.

> **But it is actually a human miracle: People work in horrible conditions for very low wages. 'Be careful,' I told them. 'You are going to be the highest-cost producer, because this human miracle is not going to last.'** [8]

Closely related to unresolved tensions are systemic inequities, disparities that privilege some while disadvantaging others, causing those on the outside to feel marginalised or exploited, until a tipping point is reached and the inevitable blowback occurs. Examples of these powder keg situations exploding include the Arab Spring of 2010–11, the London riots of 2011 and the Occupy Wall Street movement of 2011. Common causes included dissatisfaction with governing institutions and leaders, widening economic and social disparities, and generational unemployment and poverty. Such systemic inequity is not confined to human causes, nor are the responses necessarily revolutionary, as we've seen with the sustained rise of the animal rights movement in recent decades.

Looking forward, intergenerational tensions are sure to continue to rise given the inequitable systems that privilege older voters while disadvantaging younger and future generations, particularly with regard to tax benefits, housing affordability and climate change policies.

EXPOSING SYSTEMIC INEQUITIES

As the Pierre Wack insight demonstrates, systemic inequities rarely appear obvious to those who benefit most from them. If the current system works well for them, they will have little incentive to change the way things are. As a consequence, change tends to come from outside the establishment, from the 'Bedouins knocking on the door, seeking power (military, cultural, financial, worker)'. [9]

Organisations that benefit from systemic inequities (such as tax breaks and barriers to entry) should always be conscious that their fortune is merely a result of artificial intervention and that just as the Lord giveth, the Lord can taketh away.

Considerations for the anticipatory organisation include:

- Who or what is marginalised or exploited by current policies?
- What events might cause these systemic inequities to reach a tipping point?
- Who outside of power is prepared to persist for their cause?

5. Slow-burning issues

Nuances matter: slow-burning issues have a habit of creeping up on inattentive organisations and societies.

'In an information-rich world,' observed economist and political scientist Herbert Simon in 1971,

> **the wealth of information means a dearth of something else: a scarcity of whatever it is that information consumes. What information consumes is rather obvious: it consumes the attention of its recipients. Hence, a wealth of information creates a poverty of attention.'[10]**

The effects of slow-burning issues build up subtly over time; stress fractures will eventually cause a break. Rising incidences of obesity, mental health problems and shortening attention spans are all examples of current slow-burning issues in the developed world.

If detected at all, such issues are often not perceived to be important, until the problem reaches a crisis point. There are three reasons for this indifference.

a. THE IMPACT OF THE ISSUE APPEARS TOO DISTANT — 'THAT'S A MATTER FOR THE FUTURE'

Early reports about the future impact of climate change presented alarming scenarios of melting glaciers, rising sea levels and displaced populations. Yet governments, industry and the public remained largely indifferent to the issue. The problem was that the impacts were forecast for decades or even centuries into the future, so they failed to ignite any significant sense of urgency. The issue was just too far away.

b. THERE IS INSUFFICIENT EVIDENCE TO SUPPORT IT — 'I DON'T SEE THAT AS AN ISSUE'

In 1954 Dr Wilhelm C. Hueper, then director of the environmental cancer section of the US National Cancer Institute, declared, 'If excessive smoking actually plays a role in the production of lung cancer, it seems to be a minor one, if judged by the evidence on hand.'[11]

The problem with slow-burning issues is that they develop too slowly. As a result, available evidence remains inconclusive and is often muddied by conflicting information and even disinformation, particularly from those whose interests are threatened. As a consequence, regulators, the public and industry tend to get caught in a no man's land of uncertainty or indifference ('Are we in a crisis or not?'), until they are overwhelmed by stealth.

c. THE RELEVANCE OF THE ISSUE IS NOT OBVIOUS — 'IT'S JUST NOT ON OUR RADAR'

In this instance, the relationship between the issue and the organisation doesn't appear obvious, which leads to a failure to attach relevance or significance to the issue.

From 1998 to 2010 the city of Melbourne endured a gangland war that claimed more than 30 lives. Yet it wasn't until the midpoint of this period that the media and state government began to sit up and take notice, and by then events had taken on a life of their own.

'Even the politicians were ducking for cover,' writes Adam Shand in his well-researched book on the gangland wars, *Big Shots*.

> **I had called the Premier Steve Bracks's press secretary and she had reacted to my interview request with a mixture of contempt and incredulity. *'Why would he want to talk about that?'* she'd asked with exaggerated emphasis. 'We'll get back to you', she said curtly, but they never did.[12]**

The very public executions of Jason Moran and his bodyguard in the front seat of a van with five children in the back at a Saturday morning junior football clinic proved the turning point in the public's perceptions of the Melbourne gangland war. This extreme event brought the issue in from the periphery and put it in the forefront of the public's consciousness. Now the killings were seen as a public safety issue, the relevance of the gangland war could no longer be denied. 'It would be nearly eight months before Premier Bracks deigned to give me an interview,' Shand recalls. 'By then it would be hard to avoid: the murders would become the only issue he was being asked to comment on.'

IDENTIFYING SLOW-BURNING ISSUES

The most effective way of detecting slow-burning issues before they emerge is to apply the pendulum theory of change.[13] Combining the theories of Pitirim Sorokin, Clare Graves and Ronald Inglehart, pendulum theory can be summarised like this:

> **Whenever we gain something, we lose something else. Over time what we lose becomes scarce, it becomes increasingly valued, and our perceptions and behaviours change accordingly, spurring future social change.**

Over the years, pendulum theory has been consistently captured in the theories and works of social scientists, macro-historians and psychologists. Why do systems have limits? In his book *Social and Cultural Dynamics*, sociologist Pitirim Sorokin explains:

> When such a system of truth and reality ascends, grows, and becomes more and more monopolistically dominant, its false part tends to grow, while its valid part tends to decrease. Becoming monopolistic or dominant, it tends to drive out all the other systems of truth and reality, and with them the valid parts they contain. At the same time, like dictatorial human beings, becoming dominant, the system is likely to lose increasingly its validities and develop its falsities. The net result of such a trend is that as the domination of the system increases, it becomes more and more inadequate.[14]

Through his long study of the levels of human existence and adult human development, professor of psychology Clare Graves approaches the cycle of change from a human values perspective.[15] 'My research,' he explains, 'indicates that man is learning that values and ways of living which were good for him at one period in his development are no longer good because of the changed condition of his existence.' Political scientist Ronald Inglehart's theory for social change is based on his scarcity hypothesis, which contends, 'An individual's priorities reflect the socioeconomic environment: one places the greatest subjective value on those things that are in relatively short supply.'[16]

Each of these theories is consistent in suggesting an oscillating pattern of change, much like a swinging pendulum. For Sorokin, it's the oscillation between different systems as the true and false parts of each system rise and fall; for Graves, it's the oscillation between different types of thinking required to solve different types of problems; and for Inglehart, it's the oscillation between abundance and scarcity that drives future social change (see figure 6.3, overleaf).

Through the theory of Sorokin, we can interpret the rising incidence of mental illness as the false part of individualism emerging. The work of Graves suggests the resource depletion and social inequity resulting from rampant materialism create problems that a new post-materialistic type of thinking will be required to solve. Finally, the hypothesis of Inglehart highlights the potential for 'busy-ness' and the loss of personal time to become drivers of future social change.

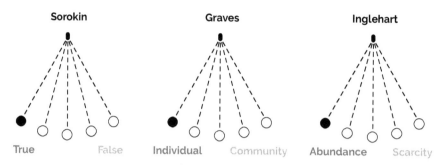

Figure 6.3: pendulum theory

The theories of Sorokin, Graves and Inglehart provide valuable tools for anticipating the emergence of embryonic issues and future social change.

Considerations for the anticipatory organisation include:

What is the price being paid for today's behaviours? (What is being lost or becoming scarce?)

Or, in the language of Sorokin:

What is the false part of the dominant paradigm?

6. Social values

In all the years that I have been studying and applying futures methods, no theory of change has proved more valuable than understanding social values and how these values evolve over time. Time and again I've found that such an understanding provides genuine insight into past, present and future behaviours.

Our social values provide a pointer to future behaviour because they influence how we *see* the world—our perception of concepts such as status, progress, time, consumption, debt, family, work, success and all other aspects of life. Our values define what we consider to be important—what we aspire to, what we prioritise, what we consider acceptable and what we reject. This then influences how we behave and the social outcomes that arise from this behaviour.

Values are important because they are deep-rooted and change only slowly over time. Unlike short-term trends or fads, shifts in our values underpin sustained social change. Clare Graves believes our values are shaped by two factors[17]:

- external *life conditions* (context)
- internal *thinking capacity* (capability).

Although age is not a determinant, there is often a substantial difference between the values of older and younger members of society, as they have been shaped by different experiences (different contexts).

The vast potential for social values as a source of insight into the future becomes obvious when we answer the following three questions:

a) Is there a hierarchy of values that individuals and societies move through? If so, what is it?

b) What conditions are required to facilitate the movement of individuals and societies along this hierarchy?

c) What themes and behaviours are individuals and societies likely to be attracted to at each stage of this hierarchy? What are they likely to reject?

Let me address each of these questions by drawing on the work of Dr Graves and Ronald Inglehart.

a. IS THERE A HIERARCHY OF VALUES THAT INDIVIDUALS AND SOCIETIES MOVE THROUGH? IF SO, WHAT IS IT?

Yes. Multiple studies of human psychological development have consistently shown that values development within individuals and across societies follows a similar hierarchy.[18] [19] [20] In the language of Inglehart, the upper levels of this hierarchy, the levels that dominate developed societies, can be expressed as[21]:

Traditional values → Materialistic values → Post-materialistic values

While the specifics of the future are impossible to predict, such a hierarchy provides insight into the general direction of social thinking and behaviour, given the prevalence of certain conditions.

b. WHAT CONDITIONS ARE REQUIRED TO FACILITATE THE MOVEMENT OF INDIVIDUALS AND SOCIETIES ALONG THIS HIERARCHY?

Inglehart and Graves agree that human values are contextual; as different conditions emerge new thinking is required to deal with the different challenges being faced. This contextual influence determines that both progressive and regressive transition along the values hierarchy is possible. For Inglehart, as mentioned earlier, transition is based on his scarcity hypothesis—namely, individuals place the greatest subjective value on those things that are in relatively short supply. Hence, social stability diminishes the need for traditional values with their emphasis on rigid laws and structures. Similarly, sustained prosperity leads to a greater emphasis on quality of life and self-expression as the desire for a higher material standard of living is satisfied.[22] 'Other things being equal,' Inglehart suggests, 'we would expect prolonged periods of high prosperity to encourage the spread of Post Materialist values; economic decline would have the opposite effect.'[23]

Not that this evolution of values is ever instantaneous. As Inglehart explains in his complementary *socialisation hypothesis*,

The relationship between socioeconomic environment and value priorities is not one of immediate adjustment: a substantial time lag is involved because, to a large extent, one's basic values reflect the conditions that prevailed during one's pre-adult years.[24]

For Graves, three of the key factors for progressive values transition are[25]:

i. *Resolution of existing problems*—for example, the transition from a materialistic to a post-materialistic outlook requires that economic wants and priorities are first satisfied ('I have enough').

ii. *Dissonance*—which occurs when issues associated with the current way of thinking and behaving begin to mount or become overwhelming. For Traditionalists, this dissonance might take the form of disillusionment with authority and an increasing desire for self-determination and self-expression. For materialists, perhaps it's a crisis of conscience as they become aware of the consequences of their behaviour (the environmental impact, for example); or they feel overwhelmed by debt or the stress and rush of their lifestyles; or perhaps it's the realisation that while they have achieved material abundance, it has come at a high cost ('It's lonely being independent').

iii. *Insight*—that an alternative way forward must be recognised to solve the new problems. In the absence of such genuine alternatives, the prevailing ways will remain.

Of course, when new insights do emerge they are rarely welcomed with open arms. Instead, a battle begins, with advocates for the established system desperate to maintain the status quo, and advocates for the emerging system equally insistent on another way. These transitional periods tend to be characterised by opposition, disinformation, contradictory signals and false dawns, until a new equilibrium is achieved.

From the theories of Inglehart and Graves, it's clear that just as the society in which we live (context) shapes our values, attitudes and behaviours, over time these behaviours create trends and events that in turn reshape our social context, thereby requiring a new set of values and behaviours to solve emergent issues, and so on (see figure 6.4, overleaf).

c. WHAT THEMES AND BEHAVIOURS ARE INDIVIDUALS AND SOCIETIES LIKELY TO BE ATTRACTED TO AT EACH STAGE OF THIS HIERARCHY? WHAT ARE THEY LIKELY TO REJECT?

During the Traditional stage, we see an emphasis on hierarchy and structure to deliver stability and order. Rules are put in place to be obeyed, superiors know best, and *children should be seen but not heard*. Traditionalists have a strong belief in higher authority and are loyal to whoever that 'authority' might be, including religious leaders, politicians, workplace managers, law enforcement officers and the military. They have a strong sense of duty and to being good citizens. They believe in discipline and playing by the rules. They accept social norms and are less likely to challenge traditional conventions, for example around work, lifestyle, marriage or gender roles.

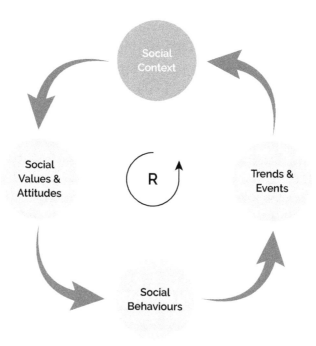

Figure 6.4: social context

Social context, values and behaviours are constantly evolving, interacting and influencing each other, driving continuous, nonlinear change.

Conventional thinking ('That's the way things are done around here'), loyalty, reliability, affordability, and sacrificing now for later reward are common themes in a society dominated by traditional values.

With the rise of Materialism, the contrast with traditional values is stark. We see the shift away from belief in authority and towards independence ('I'm smart, I know best'). From a primary concern for affordability and reliability we see a greater emphasis on superficial comparisons ('bigger, better, faster'), appealing to the materialistic mindset. In this world, the pendulum swings from loyalty to efficiency, as the focus shifts to bottom-line outcomes ('getting things done'). Resources are there to be exploited and progress is equated to growth ('It's all about the dollar').

At this level of thinking personal identity, status and success are tied up with material success ('I am what I own' or 'what I wear' or 'what I earn'). This mindset tends to be quite insecure, hence the fixation on superficial comparisons and the need to constantly prove oneself. In the mind of the Materialist, life is a competition, and rules exist to be exploited in the pursuit of winning.

From this simple sketch of the types of themes Materialists are attracted to, and the types of behaviours and objectives they prioritise, it becomes apparent just how foreseeable many of the industry and social developments of the past 30 years actually were. With their focus on superficial comparisons, marketing, advertising and packaging were always going to prosper. If you worked in retail, fashion, motor vehicles or manufacturing, then the age of materialism was always going to be your moment in the sun. A belief that 'bigger is better' underpinned a shift in the housing sector that led to the 'McMansion' trend and Australian houses becoming the biggest in the world, despite families having fewer children. In a 'busy' world where everyone is trying to compete, caffeine becomes society's preferred legal drug of choice because you need energy and you need to be alert. And of course, materialism is a godsend for the finance sector because the whole system relies on funding and credit.

And what about the flipside of this mindset, the predictable negative aspects that would slowly build to create the overwhelming dissonance necessary for a future change in thinking and behaviour? The rise of individualism and independence created a lonelier world. The cost of busy-ness included longer work hours and loss of personal time. Greater debt and insecurity and constant comparison to others meant a Materialist society was always going to be more stressed and anxious than its predecessor.

The mental health issues facing many Western societies today, and the environmental challenges brought on by the sustained exploitation of natural resources, are natural consequences of rampant materialism. And these issues are laying the foundation for the emergence of a new type of thinking.

Just as materialistic values have had such an influence in shaping society over recent decades, post-materialistic thinking is poised to make a similar impact in the coming years and decades. With post-materialism, sustainability takes priority over growth at any cost as the natural response to growing environmental awareness ('less is more'). And we see several other important pendulum swings: from rampant individualism to more community-oriented values; from competition to collaboration; from ownership to access; from consumption to creativity.

Whereas the rise of materialism delivered the age of want, post-materialism is ushering in the decline of material want, with quality replacing quantity as the measure of a successful lifestyle. This is accompanied by a type of personal liberation in the form of a greater sense of identity that comes from within, as opposed to the insecurity that comes with constantly proving yourself to others. Needless to say, those industries that have benefited most from the growth in materialistic values face a far rockier future and will need to repurpose their proposition in order to thrive in a new social values epoch.

Awareness of the sequence in which social values develop, the conditions that facilitate a shift in these values, and the different attitudes and behaviours that might emerge provides a significant framework for anticipating the future. Considerations for the anticipatory organisation therefore include:

- What are today's dominant values, and how are they influencing current behaviours and priorities?
- What events or conditions might cause these values to evolve in the future?
- What different themes and behaviours are likely to become prominent as a new set of values emerge?

A summary of these first six techniques for identifying and anticipating the emergence of embryonic issues and opportunities appears in table 6.1.

Table 6.1: embryonic issues — a summary table

Category	The issue exists but …	Framework for anticipation
Dirty secrets	The public don't know about the issue.	Which practices are the public unaware of, *but if they were*, it would alter their perception of who we are and what we do?
Cultural hypocrisies	The public don't see the issue.	What cultural hypocrisies underpin our operations or performance?
		What events might cause the public to overcome their paradigm blindness with regard to these hypocrisies?
		How can we manage our operations to prevent these events from occurring?

(continued)

Table 6.1: embryonic issues — a summary table *(cont'd)*

Category	The issue exists but …	Framework for anticipation
Unresolved tensions	The public don't like the issue.	**Internal** What are the frustrations customers have with our products or services? What roadblocks do our processes or regulations put in the way of the customer's experience? What unnecessary margins can others target? Do we give our customers a reason to stay? **External** Which issues are tolerated that are universally disliked or drive people to despair? Which issues have the potential to emerge as unresolved tensions in the future?
Systemic inequities	The public don't want to know about the issue.	Who or what is marginalised or exploited by current policies? What events might cause these systemic inequities to reach a tipping point? Who outside of power is prepared to persist for their cause?

Slow-burning issues	The public don't care about the issue.	What is the price being paid for today's behaviours? (What is being lost or becoming scarce?)
		What is the *false* part of the dominant paradigm?
Social values	The public are the issue.	What are today's dominant values, and how are they influencing current behaviours and priorities?
		What events or conditions might cause these values to evolve in the future?
		What different themes and behaviours are likely to become prominent as a new set of values emerge?

7. Scenarios

Without doubt the most effective technique for anticipating and preparing for future discontinuities is scenario planning. Scenarios are effective for identifying both external and internal opportunities as they help managers to reperceive the external world and to reconceive their internal operations. Part III of this book describes in comprehensive detail the process of developing and applying scenarios, empowering the reader with the resources to implement their own anticipatory strategic design process.

PART III
DOING

CHAPTER 7

The strategic challenge

Proficiency at strategic design is an internal capability that is difficult to replicate

The fluidity of change ensures that a strategic outlook can never be 'a magic formula for success for all time'.[1] Over time, the advantages that flow from having a market-leading strategy are diminished by shifting market conditions or the innovation of competitors—hence the need to continually develop new and distinct strategies to thrive in a constantly changing environment.

This need for ongoing strategic transformation shifts the internal emphasis from developing a one-time best strategy to designing the best strategy process. In turn, proficiency at strategic design becomes what David Teece calls a dynamic capability, an internal process delivering strategic value that is difficult to imitate. With such proficiency, volatile conditions become your preferred environment and uncertainty provides the basis for a sustained competitive edge. This is the strategic advantage delivered by scenarios.

In chapter 4 I introduce an integrated and dynamic process for strategy development specifically designed to optimise organisational performance in an uncertain and turbulent environment. At the core of this process sits scenario planning. Part III describes this strategy process in detail, with each chapter corresponding to the relevant components of the process shown in figure 7.1.

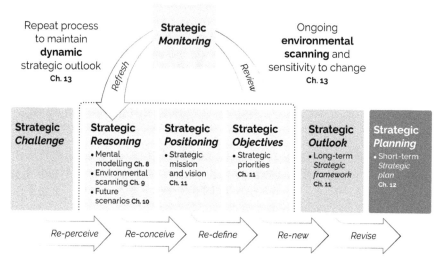

Figure 7.1: an integrated and dynamic strategy process

As the organisation develops its capabilities for anticipating environmental changes and generating internal renewal, ongoing volatility is welcomed as the gateway to step changes in performance.

Typically, the strategy development component of this process, incorporating the building of future scenarios and culminating in the design of a long-term strategic framework and shorter-term strategic plan, takes approximately six months to complete. An indicative timeline for this process is presented as figure 7.2.

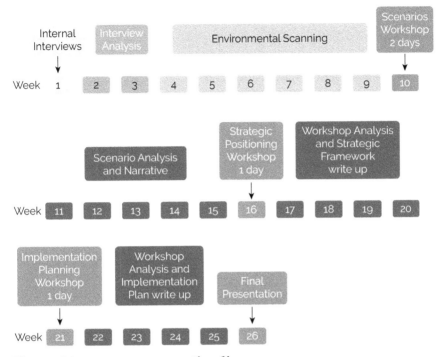

Figure 7.2: strategy process timeline

An effective scenario process involves a mix of 'hands-on' workshop facilitation and 'hands-off' analysis and reflection; getting this mix right is a key to generating fresh insights.

Getting to work

Effective scenarios are designed to address a *strategic challenge*—any pressing issue the organisation considers strategically significant. These challenges can relate to strategic positioning ('What could we be?'), future investment or innovation ('What should we do?') or concerns about an emerging issue with potential implications ('What could be the future of ... ?'). Whichever form the strategic challenge takes, it must be owned by internal management, the ultimate users of the scenario output, and it must represent their key priorities or concerns about the future.

It's worth emphasising just how important the strategic challenge and its relevance to key decision makers is. From here on, all activities and decisions pertain to the strategic challenge—it sits at the centre of the scenario planning process.

Organisations typically face three types of strategic challenge in which the use of scenarios is advantageous: *innovative, specific* and *exploratory*.

Innovative strategic challenges relate to the organisational need for insights. In this instance, the need for action has been identified, but the course of action has yet to be determined. These types of challenges can be as broad and transformational as defining the corporation's future strategic positioning and objectives, or as narrow as identifying future product opportunities:

- 'How do we position our business for sustained future success?'
- 'What products or services might customers want in the future?'

Specific strategic challenges relate to a particular proposed activity:

- 'Should we purchase a California winery?'
- 'Should we invest in greater production capacity?'

These challenges tend to carry the unspoken assumptions and expectations of a business-as-usual future, presupposing similar market conditions and demand. Scenarios test the validity of these assumptions and expectations, as is discussed in chapter 9.

Exploratory strategic challenges relate to a knowledge gap about an emerging area of interest or concern—'We need to know more about…' or 'What are we doing about…?'

These scenarios are particularly useful when an issue is emerging, but its development remains uncertain and its future impact unclear. The challenge in this instance is to improve understanding of the issue's development and relevance while there is still time to manage your response. Examples could include:

- 'What might be the impact of climate change on international migration and national security?'

- 'How might online gaming affect physical gambling venues in the future?'

The outcomes of these scenarios then provide a framework that can lead either to direct strategic action or to the development of more focused decision scenarios.

Setting the scenario horizon

The scenario horizon relates directly to the strategic challenge. It represents the time frame you're interested in planning for—how far into the future you want to explore. Agreeing on this horizon is one of the first activities of the scenario process, and it's also likely to be the first topic of debate. Almost always the organisation's managers will push for a shorter time period—a horizon of 5 years rather than 10, or 10 years rather than 20.

This push reflects their conditioning to short-term thinking and goals, their desire for immediate action and their scepticism about the long-term future. Managers who have not been involved in a scenario process before will naturally equate the scenario horizon with a timeline for action; in other words, a long-term horizon equates to a lack of short-term consequence. Hence, a shorter time frame suits their need for action now. In fact, effective scenarios always generate insights with actionable implications for the firm in both the short and long term.

In my experience clients are always grateful for having been pushed to a longer time horizon. Having gone through the process, they can see the benefits the longer time span provided in opening up strategic options for their organisation.

It depends on the needs of the client, of course, but my preference is for a minimum horizon of 10 years. It's the perfect length of time for participants to contemplate significant and plausible external and internal change, without losing them in the murkiness of a too distant future. For strategic transformation, with its significant operational and cultural implications, I suggest a time frame of 10 years as a minimum requirement.

Having said that, choosing a scenario horizon can be a somewhat arbitrary exercise, so here are some criteria to consider:

1. RESPONSE

$$\frac{\text{Scenario horizon}}{\text{Time required to adapt}} > 1$$

The horizon year should naturally be greater than the lead time required for the business to respond[2]. Organisations in industries with longer lead times (mining, construction, manufacturing) will naturally require more distant horizons than, say, your typical consumer goods producer. In the automotive industry, for example, where years might elapse between a vehicle's concept design and market launch, a minimum 10-year horizon would be required for the scenarios to be organisationally useful. Shell have routinely produced scenarios looking beyond 20 years since the 1970s. Concerned as they are with the transitioning global energy market, their latest set looks out to the year 2100.

2. SHADOW

Understanding the shadow of your decision takes into account the time period over which you want your decisions to remain relevant. For a *specific* strategic challenge that involves investment in long-term infrastructure, there's no point making a significant commitment in time, money and resources for the longer term, only to see your efforts made redundant by social, technological or regulatory change in the shorter term.

3. CREATIVITY AND ENGAGEMENT

The horizon year should allow enough time for participants to consider significant future change, to overcome any attachment to today's paradigms ('I can see how this could change') and to creatively engage with the exercise.

This requires a balancing act.

In the minds of most people, *distance equals difference*, so shorter time frames can restrict the amount of change participants are willing to entertain ('I can see how change could occur, but not within the next five years'). The time horizon therefore affects 'the range of movement and creativity within the scenario'.[3]

On the other hand, horizons that are too distant can disengage participants from the start, undermining the process before it begins. In this instance, the future may appear irrelevant ('It's too far away'), too uncertain ('Anything could happen') or too futuristic ('Where are the flying cars?').

A means to an end

When all is said and done, the horizon year is merely a disposable marker. Once your scenarios have been developed, the time horizon loses its relevance. It's the future insights generated by the process that are important: the direction and scope of change, the events and outcomes that might lead to such change, and the implications for your business. Whether you used a 5-year or a 20-year horizon to unlock these insights is not important. The insights are.

The search for these insights begins with a series of internal conversations.

How do I know what I think until I see what I say?

Strategy represents the organisation's response to its perceived future environments

'What is the main purpose of thinking?' asks lateral thinking pioneer Edward de Bono in his book *Thinking Course*.[1] 'The main purpose of thinking is to abolish thinking.'

Huh?

It's true. Once we learn and become proficient with a new skill, we tend to *switch the brain off*. Consider an experienced driver and their daily ritual of driving to a local café for their morning coffee. It's a routine they know so well: the route they'll take, how busy the traffic will be, where they'll park when they arrive. On such a simple trip, the chances are their mind is concentrating on *everything but* their driving. They are barely aware of checking their mirrors and speed and making other routine adjustments as they switch between radio stations or work on defrosting the windscreen. Because the driver is unconsciously competent at this familiar activity, thinking, to any great degree, is not really required.

Now compare that effortless experience with that of a learner driver. The novice checks all mirrors before setting off, consciously drives below the speed limit and indicates to turn a full 60 metres before reaching the intersection. The novice is alert to the slightest deviations in conditions. The act of driving is all about conscious concentration; it is all about thinking.

These examples of unconscious and conscious competence are represented in the *four stages of competence* learning model illustrated in figure 8.1.

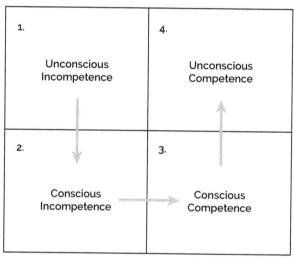

Figure 8.1: the four stages of competence model

The four stages of competence learning model shows the journey from paradigm ignorance to paradigm expertise.

In stage 1 of the model, *unconscious incompetence*, the individual is unaware of or does not acknowledge their learning or skill deficiency. In stage 2, *conscious incompetence*, the individual recognises their learning deficit and seeks to address it. In stage 3, *conscious competence*, the individual has learned the new knowledge; however, conscious effort is still required to execute the skill (as illustrated by the novice driver in the example). In the final stage of this learning model, *unconscious competence*, the individual has become proficient in the new skill and execution is 'second nature'; other tasks can now be performed simultaneously as applied thinking is no longer necessary.

And here's the relevance for organisations. Senior managers tend to be industry experts; they are unconsciously competent at what they do. They are able to deal reflexively with routine challenges in their industry because they know the dynamics and patterns so well. But the danger of leaving this unconscious competence unchecked is complacency, which John Addy has proposed as stage 5 of the learning cycle[2].

Unlike advancement through earlier stages of the learning cycle, the move to complacency is not deliberate, but is rather the result of intellectual laziness; you unconsciously drift into complacency (see figure 8.2, overleaf). You start to take things for granted, make assumptions about your industry that have become outdated and miss the significance of subtle shifts. Unwittingly you keep doing the same thing despite the fact that your environment has changed. Complacency is the stepping-stone to experiencing change as disruption.

Within corporations, familiarity with context (industry dynamics) or past success is often a recipe for complacency. This complacency, in turn, leads to a perception gap forming between the organisation's perceived reality (strategic outlook) and actual reality; any resultant business strategy will no longer *fit* with the external environment. If the business is not conscious of its institutional mental model, this widening gap can go unnoticed until it eventually affects performance.

The purpose of corporate mental modelling[3] is to prevent this strategic disharmony from occurring, to keep the organisation's perception gap at a minimum. In this respect, mental modelling is akin to sharpening a knife on a stone or tuning an instrument: it constantly hones the organisation's perceptions. So rather than abolishing thinking, mental modelling actually maintains organisational thinking and learning, keeping its strategic perceptions sharp and its strategic actions relevant.

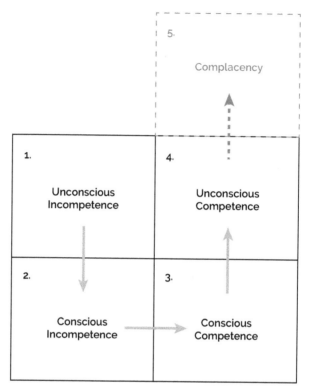

Figure 8.2: complacency, the fifth stage of the competence model

Left unchecked, unconscious competence can subtly drift into complacency, laying the foundation for strategic disruption.

The corporate mental model

Anthropologist Mary Catherine Bateson captures the important role of mental models in her observation: 'Any organism acts not in response to external reality (whatever that may be) but in response to an internally constructed version of that reality after available information has passed through a series of filters'.[4]

For a corporation, this *internally constructed version of reality* represents a subset of those of its members[5] (see figure 8.3). Often this internal view develops informally; a catchy phrase or metaphor starts at the top then works its way through to the organisation's lower levels like a slow-moving tsunami, repeated ad nauseam in presentations, meetings and corridor conversations until it becomes a natural and subconscious part of the organisation's shared language.

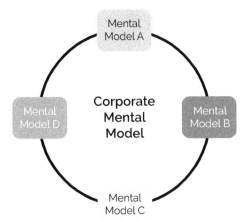

Figure 8.3: understanding the corporate mindset

Mental modelling extracts and constructs the corporate mindset, which is a subset of those of its key decision makers.

Peter Senge has pointed out that mental models are dangerous when they are tacit — when they exist below the level of awareness.[6] Because management are unaware of their mental models, the models remain unexamined. And because they are unexamined, they remain unchanged even as the world around them changes.

Mental modelling, on the other hand, is a formal process for understanding just what these internal perspectives are. This involves extracting and interpreting the perceptions, assumptions and priorities of key decision makers — *What is our purpose? What do we think is happening? What do we think could happen? What do we want to know?* This articulation of the organisation's mindset is ground zero for scenario building. It provides an understanding of why the company acts as it does today, an insight into how it might act tomorrow, and a framework for future research and exploration.

Articulating mental models

Internal interviews have proven to be an invaluable tool for extracting and understanding how managers *see* the future. For the interviewee, this process allows them to briefly step away from operational concerns of the day-to-day to reflect on what they think and why. This reflection often induces a deeper perspective as the respondent is allowed the time for critical internal examination.

For the interviewer, these 'strategic conversations'[7] provide a window into the minds of management—an understanding of the perceptions, assumptions and issues that occupy the upper levels of the organisation.

For the scenario planner, the conversations achieve several significant outcomes:

1. **Buy-in.** They involve relevant parties (decision makers and end users) in the scenario and strategy development from the outset.

2. **Relevance.** They ensure the scenarios address the key concerns of decision makers. Interviews can help to define or refine the strategic challenge and its surrounding issues, tying exploration of the future back to today's managerial priorities and concerns.

3. **Structure.** They provide a framework for subsequent environmental scanning and research.

4. **Insight.** They often expose the interviewer to nuggets of insight that prove invaluable as the strategic design process unfolds (as discussed in the next section).

5. **Orientation.** They are the perfect vehicle for expedited learning, providing a rich background on the organisation and industry that is particularly useful for external interviewers with a limited knowledge of either.

To optimise buy-in to the strategy development and future implementation, it's important that as many internal interviews as is practical are conducted. My experience is that between 15 and 20 interviews is sufficient to expose the interviewee to the range and quality of information required to take the strategy process forward. Typically, these interviews last between an hour and 90 minutes.

Who should be interviewed depends on the strategic challenge being addressed. Ask yourself: Who are the key people whose insights and involvement are significant to the successful development and implementation of this strategy? Each of the interviewees should also be involved in all subsequent stages of the strategic design process.

'THAT'S RIDICULOUS!'

During the interviews you will be exposed to a number of themes (language, metaphors, trends, forecasts, clichés) that emerge consistently across the respondents and typically reflect the informal corporate mindset. Perhaps more important than these recurring themes are the rarer 'nuggets of insight' that capture your attention because of the different perspective they provoke. These information outliers should be recorded with enthusiasm as they offer a rich source of insight that can play a pivotal role in future scenario and strategy development.

In an interview for the 2030 public libraries project mentioned briefly in chapter 4 (and discussed further in chapter 11), the respondent, having just returned from a study tour in Scandinavia, spoke of libraries with recording studios as a possible future direction for Victorian libraries. For an outsider to the industry, this concept was so foreign that I distinctly remember thinking to myself, *That'll never happen*. After all, weren't libraries essentially about peace and quiet? Yet his remarks stayed with me, and after the development of two scenarios for 2030, one of which featured increased community interest in creativity, my 'a-ha' moment arrived. I could now see a strategic fit between libraries and recording studios that I hadn't recognised before.

The future strategic positioning for the 'creative library' was now very much alive in my head. And while it was the scenarios that helped me to see the role of public libraries in a different light, they had actually helped me to reap what the interviews had sown.

In an earlier interview for the same project, the recent failed implementation of a bookless library was mentioned. Once again, the idea of a library without books was so hard to comprehend that I immediately thought to myself, *Of course the library failed—it had no books!* Still, the novelty of the concept and the jolt of my initial reaction registered with me.

The second scenario created in this project highlighted the social need for dynamic learning. Digital transformation had disrupted multiple traditional industries, leaving redundant employees to ask, 'Where do I fit in?' In this scenario, the opportunity opened up for public libraries to become hubs of community learning. I now understood how libraries could no longer be *just* about books. Again, while the subsequent strategic positioning of the 'community library' as an active learning environment was a result of these scenario insights, the concept was born out of the earlier interview process.

'WHAT INFLAMES YOU?'[8]

So how do you recognise when interview responses are potentially insightful or significant? You note your reaction. When you hear a response that sounds novel, or counterintuitive, or even *ridiculous*, jot it down. A good rule of thumb for identifying information that has potential significance for the future is to check whether it triggers a light bulb (*a-ha!*) moment or prompts your instant dismissal ('That'll never happen'). It's the novelty of the perspective you're hearing that drives both these extremes. This contrasts with the usual effect when responses are common or mainstream ('I've already heard that'). This technique may not be scientific, but if the interviewee's comments trigger a strong internal reaction, make sure you record their words.

Structuring the conversations

The Institute for the Future is credited with pioneering the design of future-oriented questions to inform strategic planning. These questions were purposefully broad to encourage expansive conversation, as opposed to formal interrogation: 'The purpose of the interview design is to allow respondents an opportunity to identify any development they choose, in the belief that, if the development is important enough to them, it will arise in one context or another.'[9]

The initial interviews conducted by the institute in the 1970s consisted of questions around the following areas:

- the interrogation of the 'clairvoyant'
- a report on an unfavourable future environment
- a report on a favourable future environment
- the identification of future decisions to be made
- the identification of current management assumptions about the future environment.[10]

These questions were then picked up by Pierre Wack and his team of scenario planners at Shell, who subsequently moulded their own version based largely on the Institute for the Future's design.[11] Shell's additional questions related to[12]:

- lessons from the past
- constraints in the system
- managerial legacy.

Regardless of the number or type of questions you ask, I suggest you adopt the same approach as Shell and tailor the conversation to the needs and constraints of your organisation. As much as possible the interviews should be open-ended, with general questions intended to 'trigger a conversation'[13], as opposed to working rigorously through a linear set of specific questions that shut down expansive thinking.

Having said that, here is a list of questions from which I regularly draw for innovative strategic challenges, such as 'How do we position our business for sustained future success?' Collectively these questions will create a comprehensive picture of an organisation's strategic outlook, covering domains such as corporate identity, hopes and fears (strategic positioning), assumptions and expectations about the future (strategic reasoning), and priorities, constraints and sacred cows (strategic objectives).

These questions draw a great deal from earlier work by the Institute for the Future and the scenario planning team at Shell. Given the conversational style of the interview and the likely overlap in responses, six to eight questions in a single interview should be more than enough to capture the insights you are seeking:

1. 'How would you define the role or purpose of your organisation?'

2. 'Which external factors are having, or could have, a significant influence on your response to the strategic challenge?'

3. 'In relation to the strategic challenge, what significant developments do you expect to occur in the future?'

4. 'How might alternative expectations for the future differ from your own?'

5. 'In relation to the strategic challenge, what are the three things you would most like to know about the future?'

6. 'What does a prosperous / less than prosperous future for your organisation look and feel like?'

7. 'What are the major decisions on your planning horizon?'

8. 'What internal or external constraints present a challenge to future organisational change?'

9. 'Which events from the past, either internal or external, provide important lessons for the future?'

10. 'Are there any aspects of your business that you feel are sacred cows or "untouchables"?'

11. 'What are the unwritten rules that guide decision making and behaviour within your organisation?'

12. 'When you move on from your role, what is it you would like to leave behind or be remembered for?'

In my experience, greater value is extracted from these sessions if the respondents receive an outline of the questions before their interview.

It should also be noted that the relevant scenario horizon would always be agreed before the interview takes place.

Interpreting the conversations

1. IDENTITY

How would you define the role or purpose of your organisation?

I always start my interviews with this question ('What business are you in?'). It seeks to understand how broad or narrow are the boundaries the interviewee places around the organisation's identity—*What's in play and what's not?* These perceptual boundaries frame the questions managers ask about the future, where they look for signals of change and the relevance they attach to such signals.

As the interviewer, you should be sensitive to narrow perceptions that limit the organisation's ability to adapt to external changes or to detect relevance in social change. Generally, the more specific the response, the narrower the organisation's sense of identity ('We are a car company').

Likewise, be aware of broader descriptions of identity ('We are in the mobility business…') that are inconsistent with the organisation's operations ('…but we only make cars'). In this second instance, the organisation is likely doing itself a disservice by limiting its operations to such a narrow focus—while it talks the talk, it's yet to walk the walk.

Both of these examples provide your earliest leverage for future strategic change.

2. INFLUENCING FACTORS

Which external factors are having, or could have, a significant impact on your response to the strategic challenge?

The purpose here is to get respondents to look beyond their organisation and articulate the external factors and trends they are paying attention to. These factors can be within the organisation's immediate industry or transactional environment (retailer consolidation, for example) or in the broader social or contextual environment (such as growing public distrust in institutions). The focus, however, must be on those factors outside the organisation's direct control.

The answers provided to this question are likely to be a function of how broadly the interviewee sees the role of the organisation (refer to question 1). Consequently, this question is effective for revealing corporate *blind spots*—those external issues that are not identified or are underestimated because they're not considered relevant to the company's future.

A key point to remember here is that as the interviewer, it is important not to prompt the respondent; you are seeking their *top of mind* interests.

3. EXPECTATIONS

In relation to the strategic challenge, what significant developments do you expect to occur in the future?

In addressing this question, respondents expose you to the future they expect to unfold, the future they are currently planning for. In close-knit organisations or industries, this question tends to draw the most convergent responses, to the point where a rich and consistent picture of the 'official future' usually emerges.

Listening to the future expectations of managers is an effective way of surfacing assumptions and uncovering future vulnerabilities. The interviewer should pay particular attention to the assumptions that have to be realised for these expectations to eventuate. Testing which of these assumptions are particularly fragile then becomes the purpose of the scanning and research phase that follows.

You should also be sensitive to inconsistencies such as expectations that are based on tradition and the past, as opposed to the impact of external influencing factors previously identified (refer to question 2).

Examples of common expectations include:

- *Conditions will soon return to normal* ('The current downturn is just a blip').
- *The good times will roll on* ('I can't imagine that ever happening to our industry').
- *The future will be much like the past* ('I expect our business to continue steady as she goes').
- *History repeats itself* ('This industry is cyclical. It's our turn at the top now, but the wheel will turn').

4. ASSUMPTIONS

How might alternative expectations for the future differ from your own?

I particularly like this question as a follow-up, because it's specifically designed to prompt the respondent to reflect on their own assumptions and to be explicit about their reasons for discounting alternate futures.

For the interviewer, this question should provide insights into:

- the respondent's awareness of alternate futures ('What else could happen?')
- why the respondent feels these alternate futures are unlikely, invalid or not a concern ('I don't think that will happen because … ')
- the respondent's blind spots, lack of sensitivity or biases[14] ('Where aren't they looking?'; 'Where are they vulnerable?').

5. UNCERTAINTIES

In relation to the strategic challenge, what are the three things you would most like to know about the future?

This question is designed to draw out those issues the interviewee considers to be both uncertain and significant. Why only three? Well, as Kees van der Heijden writes, this limit introduces the concept of relative impact[15]: 'There is much uncertainty in the business environment and it is useful to encourage the interviewee to reflect on what is really going to make a difference.'

6. HOPES AND FEARS

What does a prosperous / less than prosperous future for your organisation look and feel like?

The question about a positive future brings out the interviewee's values and goals, encouraging them to reflect on the future they want for the organisation, and what's required to enable that future to develop. On the flipside, the question about a less than prosperous future elicits their fears, requiring reflection on the future they want to avoid.

These questions are powerful because they go to the heart of the strategic exercise by making explicit what's at stake ('If we can solve this challenge, then this is the prosperity that awaits us'; 'If we don't act soon, our future is bleak').

In my experience, this set of questions tends to produce rich responses as the interviewee brings to life what different visions of the future mean to them. The interviewee should be encouraged to go into as much detail as possible, providing a sense of what the organisation *feels* like in the future, as well as what it does.

In an interview for the 2030 public libraries project, I received a response that provided such detail. The respondent described her vision of a failed future, a future in which public libraries were neglected, having failed to adapt to the changing needs of society. Her description of tiny decaying buildings with broken windows, and sparse book collections covered with dust and cobwebs made real the consequences of losing public relevance and government support.

In the responses to these questions, the interviewer should take particular note of how these different futures might come about. What decisions and opportunities were or were not taken? What events influenced the different outcomes?

7. PRIORITIES

What are the major decisions on your planning horizon?

This question draws out the organisation's strategic priorities. Responses to this question may or may not comprise the specific strategic challenge; however, they do provide further focus for future scenario exploration ('What else can the scenarios help with?').

Including responses to this question in subsequent research and scenario development broadens the relevance of the exercise and ensures a more holistic strategic response.

8. CONSTRAINTS

What internal or external constraints present a challenge to future organisational change?

This question seeks to identify the internal or external pressures that challenge the organisation's capacity to adapt—'What keeps the current system in place?' These constraints may be financial, political, legal, cultural, historical, technological or physical (infrastructure, geography).

Examples include:

- social pressure on governments to maintain public schools, swimming pools or libraries
- political pressure to prop up local industries, achieve a budget surplus or increase the quota of underrepresented parties in institutions
- union pressure on wages and conditions, or shareholder pressure on dividend returns.

Financial constraints in particular are a familiar story in business, and are not necessarily due to a lack of funds. Just as common is the scenario of an organisation feeling beholden to an overly generous benefactor, or a business with an unhealthy reliance on a narrow income stream. Such reliance acts as a constraint in that it tends to lock in existing behaviour at the expense of pursuing alternate strategies. In this instance, the product or service to which the organisation is tied is deemed *too big to fail*.

Sometimes the past decisions of current management can act as a constraint. This is not necessarily because these decisions physically lock the organisation into pursuing a certain path, but because there is too much at stake for management to change tack. In these instances, when turning back is not seen as an option, the CEO tends to adopt a *crash-through or crash* mentality ('We've come too far to go back now').

Gaining an understanding of what an organisation's constraints are, then testing their legitimacy (are they real or perceived?) can be one of the challenges in a scenarios exercise.

9. PAST EVENTS

Which events from the past, either internal or external, provide important lessons for the future?

Often high-profile failures or successes create a legacy that outlasts their usefulness. These events from the past become organisational 'truths', infiltrating the minds of managers, passed down through the years, and often recited as a way of justifying a position ('We tried that years ago and it didn't work' or 'Remember when...').

Past events can burn themselves into the organisation's psyche, preventing it from taking advantage of opportunities or sensing threats from competitors ('They won't try that'). The interviewer should be sensitive to these events, acknowledging that they occurred in a different historical context that may hold little current truth. Sometimes it's all about timing, as Foster's discovered with its various attempts to establish a lite beer category in the Australian alcohol market.

Lower carb or 'lite' beers had been very popular in the United States for decades. Looking to replicate this success, Australian beer companies made several attempts at launching similar products into the local market in the mid 1990s and early 2000s.

In 1995, Foster's (Carlton & United Breweries at the time) launched Diamond Draft. Despite substantial marketing efforts, the consumer response was utterly underwhelming, ensuring a short product life span.

Another effort three years later, Carlton LJ (low joule), was even less successful, leading to the widespread perception that a low-carb beer could never work in Australia—local beer drinkers were just too different culturally from their American counterparts. In one marketing manager's opinion, 'Consumers don't care about calories when they drink beer.' (Note that at this time no mainstream Australian beers carried nutritional labelling.)

It was against this background that Foster's made a third attempt in the low-carb category in 2004 with Pure Blonde. Except this time, beer drinkers were ready. Obesity was now recognised as a health crisis, and the legendary Australian beer gut was no longer a badge of honour. Carson Kressley and his mates were teaching men across the world how to dress and groom via their hit TV show *Queer Eye for the Straight Guy*, and Dr Atkins' low-carb diet was all the rage. For Australians, low-carb beer was an idea whose time had come.

Despite the changing social zeitgeist, however, the idea still received strong internal pushback from those outside the project team. The attitude of 'We've already tried that' was particularly on display when a colleague, acting as a liaison between Marketing and Sales, presented the new product to the sales team. Time and again he was forced to defend the brand's positioning as the product was howled down by the twice-bitten sales reps.

Pure Blonde went on to exceed initial sales forecasts and quickly established itself as one of Australia's fastest growing brands. In doing so, it pioneered the low-carb category for mainstream Australia, a category that today continues to be a substantial market segment. It appears that beer drinkers did care about their waistlines after all; it was just that on previous occasions the company's timing was out.

10. SACRED COWS

Are there any aspects of your business that you feel are sacred cows or 'untouchables'?

Some icons are powerful symbols that management considers 'we can't do without'. These sacred cows are often company symbols that have been associated with past success (large cars at Ford, for example). They can be products, services, logos, processes, people, structures or relationships.

Perceptions around sacred cows are often shaped by *emotional* thinking (corporate identity, traditional loyalty, symbolism) as opposed to *rational* thinking (an idea whose time has passed). There is a lot of the taken for granted in company icons — it's simply assumed they will or must continue, which is why sacred cows are always ripe areas for disruption.

They should always be approached with care, though. Often they need to be reframed in a way that enables people to consider them in a new and different light. Effective reframing allows people and organisations to move beyond the artificial constraints that sacred cows often become.

Reframing sacred cows

One of the best examples of reframing a sacred cow that I've heard was provided by Collingwood Football Club president Eddie McGuire. Preparing to face a hostile room full of Collingwood members in the late 1990s, even Eddie, a man known for his personal confidence, must have been nervous. He was about to put forward the board's case for moving the football club away from their traditional ground at Victoria Park to more spacious and modern facilities in the heart of Melbourne. This was a move sure to stir up an emotional response from the assembled masses.

His first words were a question: 'Hands up who still lives in the same house they grew up in?' His analogy was a powerful one. In an instant Eddie had reframed the thinking of his audience. Victoria Park would always be their spiritual home, but the club needed to move to larger, more modern facilities to compete in a larger, more professional competition. At the end of the meeting the members accepted the board's proposal.

Today, Collingwood's facilities are recognised as being among the best in the AFL and are the envy of the competition. The club enjoys record membership and regularly plays in front of crowds of more than 70000 people at a different home venue. Yet these successes were only possible with the *vision* to see beyond their sacred cows, the *courage* to confront them and the *creativity* to reframe them in such a way that they were able to take their supporters into the future with them.

Not all companies or senior managers have these qualities.

Betting the house on the past

Several years ago I was involved with a scenario planning project for a large hospitality and entertainment business in Sydney (as I discuss further in chapter 11). Over several decades this organisation had been extremely successful on the back of poker machine takings, and management were interested in scenarios to explore options to divest their business operations into the future.

No matter how noble the intentions might be at the start of the process, scenarios can sometimes raise issues that provoke a strong emotional pushback, as proved to be the case on this occasion.

In one of the scenario teams, a club director (surprisingly the youngest board member) and a co-facilitator became embroiled in a long, heated argument over the future of poker machine legislation.

This particular scenario was driven by strong community values and increasing government intervention, and it seemed entirely plausible that taxes on gaming revenue would increase while the appeal and tolerance of such machines would decline. In such a scenario, the client would have to actively diversify its operations to compensate for a reduction in gaming takings.

This particular director refused to engage with such a scenario, however. Even within the safe surrounds of an internal workshop he could not envisage gaming taxes increasing or the appeal of poker machines declining—'That won't ever happen!' Yet to my co-facilitator, an outsider looking in, the overwhelming evidence of mounting community concerns over problem gambling appeared a likely catalyst for future poker machine reform.

By refusing to entertain a future scenario because it challenged a sacred cow, the director was in fact denying the opportunity to learn and explore alternate strategic options. And in doing so, he was doing his organisation a major disservice.

As a postscript to this story, several years later the Australian Labor government entered an agreement to introduce mandatory pre-commitment legislation targeting problem gamblers. The gaming industry was caught completely unawares by this development; almost overnight they saw a large portion of their revenue from intensive gambling coming under threat. Their response was an aggressive, year-long, multimillion-dollar campaign, which ultimately proved successful when the Labor government broke its commitment.

My client, indeed the entire industry, had dodged a bullet. However, not all industries have the financial or political muscle required to hold back or temporarily stall social change. This is why acknowledging sacred cows and the false expectations about the future they can sometimes generate can be such a critical aspect of the scenarios process.

11. PARADIGMS

What are the unwritten rules that guide decision making and behaviour within your organisation?

This question targets the paradigms that guide behaviours within the organisation. It's a question that should cause the interviewee to reflect on the undocumented set of rules that govern their thinking and the way they see the world. According to futurist Willis Harman, 'a dominant paradigm is rarely stated explicitly; it exists as unquestioned, tacit understanding that is transmitted through culture and to succeeding generations through direct experience (rather than being "taught")'.[16] And it's the unwritten and often unspoken nature of paradigms that can make them so dangerous.

Paradigms are a rich area for disruption as they cause certain behaviours to be considered either in or out of bounds, and their persistence relies upon everybody *playing by the same rules*. But of course competitors don't always play by the rules, and customers don't even know they exist!

Industry leaders in particular are loath to break paradigms that have made them successful; it's in their interests for the status quo to be maintained—'This is what we know, this is what works for us'.

The blinding influence of paradigms

In 1998 Foster's Light Ice was easily the number one selling low-alcohol beer in Australia. Its sales were declining, however. Given the history of short-term dominance by light beer brands, Foster's was looking to shore up its leadership position by introducing a complementary premium brand into its light beer portfolio, Cascade Premium Light (CPL).

Around the same time, Foster's executives became aware that their major competitor Lion Nathan was also considering introducing a new premium light beer—Hahn Premium Light (HPL). The race was on to launch to market first.

True to its positioning as a premium brand, CPL's introductory pricing was well above Light Ice's, with a recommended selling price of $29.99 (compared with $19.99 for the mainstream light beer leader). HPL, on the other hand, exhibited all the packaging cues of premium beer, except that it was priced *below* Foster's Light Ice, at $18.99, and $11 below its supposed direct competitor.

Now we had a problem. The consumer take-up of HPL was instant, with thousands of cartons selling each week. CPL sales were dismal, barely registering in the hundreds. Foster's management had effectively been blindsided by their own internal paradigms and unwritten rules.

Emergency meetings were held across the country as the blame game began. Laughably, senior management even tried to enforce an edict that employees refer to their rival's brand only as Hahn Light, dropping any reference to 'Premium'. After all, 'How can it be a premium beer if it isn't priced accordingly?'

Facing a barrage of internal criticism, Marketing attempted to justify their strategy by claiming that Lion Nathan had 'broken the rules' of premium beer, to which the Sales Vice President calmly replied, 'What rules?'

The paradox of paradigms

Hahn Premium Light went on to overtake Foster's Light Ice as the number one selling light beer brand in Australia. Cascade Premium Light was quickly repackaged and relaunched several months later at a much lower price point. And the 'unwritten rules' of premium pricing in the Australian beer market had been changed forever.

And herein lies the paradox of paradigms: while they might be hard to change, they are quick to change. Just as most of us are wedded to our ways of thinking, once we accept a different way of seeing the world, we are able to adopt and act on a different perspective very quickly.

12. LEGACY

When you move on from your role, what is it you would like to leave behind or be remembered for?

I was always amazed how whenever a new brand manager started at Foster's they seemed compelled to change things instantly. No matter that the brand they were managing had just undergone a packaging makeover, or that millions had just been spent on a new marketing campaign, the new incumbent would always want to put their stamp on things, *to create their legacy*.

Legacies are about making an impact and being recognised, two personal goals managers most aspire to achieve. Legacies are important because they give managers something they can point to and declare, 'I did that.' Just as important, they give *others* something they can point to and say, 'She [or he] did that.' They also come in handy when it's time to apply for other roles or ask for a pay rise.

The motivation to create a personal legacy can be a powerful and sometimes overriding force, one that may not always seem logical or in the best long-term interests of the organisation.

Unearthing the legacy goals of the interviewee not only provides an insight into their personal values and ambition; it can also provide a hint as to the permissible scope of the forthcoming strategy process. By outlining their ambitions, the interviewee may in fact be introducing constraints, boundaries or directions for the process. And if this person is the one paying the bills, the interviewer would be well advised to take these boundaries into consideration when framing the scenario output.

Analysing the conversations

At the conclusion of the interviews, individual notes should be analysed and results grouped into emergent themes, insights and questions. This synthesised output should help create a comprehensive picture of the existing organisational mindset (see figure 8.4, overleaf), providing a firm foundation from which to launch the next phase of the strategic design process: environmental scanning.

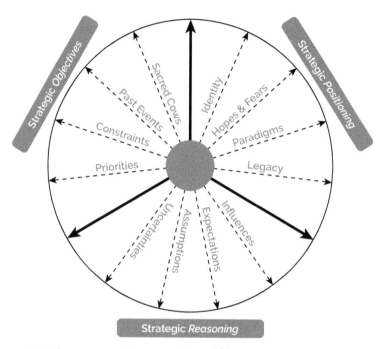

Figure 8.4: the corporate mental model

Mapping the corporate mental model provides the foundation for strategy development and the essential framework for ongoing research and scanning.

CHAPTER 9

Conversations with Mr Silly

Alternative perceptions are a great source of strategic insight

During the first week of my master's course at Swinburne University I was introduced to a quote from American philosopher Ken Wilber that would torment me with its complexity for the next two years: 'Nobody is smart enough to be wrong all the time.'[1]

It's an observation about appreciating different perspectives, or the important truths, however limited, that reside within alternative viewpoints. Just as nobody is smart enough to be 100 per cent right all the time, it's equally true that nobody is smart enough to be wrong all the time. And herein lies an essential skill for environmental scanning: the ability to seek out and engage with different points of view.

Why are alternative perceptions important? Because significant change springs from the growing acceptance and adoption of alternative or fringe perceptions.

In the 1980s Victorian Laurie Levy founded a direct action group, the Coalition Against Duck Shooting, to campaign against the recreational shooting of native waterbirds. Each year Laurie would lead a team of rescuers to Victoria's regional lakes. 'Going out to the wetlands in those days always reminded me of the Wild West in America,' he recalls. 'It was a frightening experience; birds were falling out of the sky.'[2] As a teenager in the mid 1980s I remember watching Laurie on the evening news and thinking: *Threatened by angry shooters with guns, often arrested, risking life and limb as he wades through swampland to save a few injured bird*s—*why does he bother?*

At the time, my sentiments were shared by a majority of Victorians, 75 per cent of whom were in favour of duck shooting. Laurie was seen as a troublemaker, a nuisance. After all, duck shooting had been going on forever. Laurie saw an injustice that only a minority appreciated. *How can hunting be called a sport when only one of the participants is armed?* So Laurie persisted. And slowly, thanks largely to the actions of Laurie and his supporters and allies, public perceptions turned. Today, three-quarters of Victorians *oppose* duck shooting, a complete reversal from the 1980s.

Laurie Levy is a *perception pioneer.*

Perception pioneers introduce you to a new perspective. They offer an alternative view of the world because they grasp a fundamental truth about an issue that others either can't see or don't appreciate. To the masses this truth remains hidden, sometimes in a physical sense but most often in a perceptual sense. Where others saw sport or hallowed tradition, Laurie saw carnage and injustice. While experts can tell you things you don't know, perception pioneers point out things you can't *see*; they introduce you to a new *way of seeing.*

It's their ability to overcome paradigm blindness that sets perception pioneers apart. It's important to remember that these people don't necessarily look or live differently; they simply *see* an issue differently. This is why I prefer the term 'perception pioneer' to the more commonly used 'remarkable person', introduced by Pierre Wack at Shell, which conjures up an image of someone with a special gift, when in fact they might hold an alternative view on only one particular topic.

Typical sources of new or different thinking include artists, science fiction, specialised journals, alternative media, activists and special-interest groups. But again, it's not what a person does that makes them a perception pioneer; it's how they think about and *see* a particular issue that is important.

So having conducted the internal interviews, relevant questions for environmental scanning might relate to:

- **difference**—What alternative views about the strategic challenge exist?
- **validity**—What circumstances might enable these alternative views to emerge?
- **plausibility**—How plausible are these circumstances within the scenario horizon?
- **impact**—If these views were to emerge, how might they impact responses to the strategic challenge?

Using the output from the internal interviews as a foundation, the environmental scanner can deliberately search for perceptions that challenge the organisation's orthodoxy in relation to the strategic challenge—*Who thinks differently and why?* These questions introduce a multilayered approach to scanning. On a primary level you are looking for alternative perceptions—a challenge in itself. On a secondary level you are looking for conditions, circumstances or events that might enable these alternative perceptions to emerge—*What would have to happen?* And on another, deeper level you are looking for the drivers that might shape these conditions—*Are these preconditions already in place or about to emerge?*

Two final points need to be made about the value of perception pioneers as sources of insight into the future:

1. **They are free.** They tend to offer their insights at much cheaper rates than traditional suppliers of information. Thus, you get the double benefit of richer insights at a fraction of the cost (if any).
2. **They should be integrated.** Organisations would do well to collate and cultivate their own group of perception pioneers, integrating their insights into the ongoing strategic design

process (mental modelling, scenario building). Including such people in regular forums enables managers to constantly test and refine their perceptions against those from the outside world.

Environmental scanning requires a framework

The purpose of environmental scanning is not to provide answers but to stimulate thinking. It's an input into the scenario building process that involves identifying those factors in the external environment (that is, beyond the organisation's direct control) that could really make a difference to the strategic challenge. Knowing where and how to look for these factors is critical. This is the process of environmental scanning.

Effective environmental scanning requires a framework or context to give it purpose and direction and to deliver organisational value. Before the development of scenarios, the strategic challenge and the emergent themes, insights and questions from the internal interviews provide the necessary framework for scanning. Within this framework will be a set of management *theories and queries* — theories about what could happen (expectations, assumptions) and queries about what they'd like to know (uncertainties, unknowns).

Environmental scanning seeks sources of information that:

1. challenge these theories — plausible, alternative perspectives
2. respond to these queries — address knowledge gaps.

Post-development, the scenarios provide your reference for ongoing scanning. Using the scenarios as a framework, the environmental scanner should be sensitive to signals that validate or invalidate the organisation's strategic reasoning, or signals that point to the emergence of different scenarios altogether (*reviewing*). This scanning process is then used to *refresh* the next round of strategic design, providing a continuous loop of learning, creating, adapting and monitoring, as shown in figure 9.1.

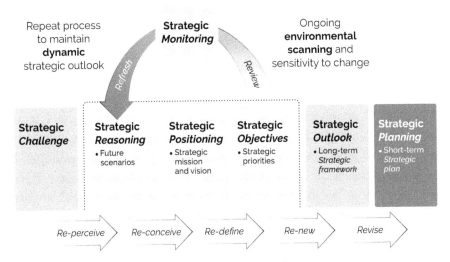

Figure 9.1: ongoing environmental scanning

Environmental scanning plays a central role at either end of the strategic design process, providing the essential stimulus for scenario building, and ongoing monitoring for signals that confirm or disconfirm the organisation's strategic reasoning.

Without these two frameworks to guide attention, the environmental scanner is destined to fail in one of three ways:

- **Paralysed by choice.** Paralysis sets in as you become overwhelmed by the sheer volume of data and information available—*Where do I start?*

- **Down the rabbit hole.** Like *Alice in Wonderland* you enthusiastically take a journey into the unknown, looking everywhere but seeing nothing, subscribing to everything but reading nothing. Eventually you are buried by the data, files and information you accumulate. And while these pieces of information might be interesting in themselves, they tend to be strategically useless, personally distracting and lacking in cohesion.

- **Organisational irrelevance.** Sure, you're busy, but the people that matter are starting to wonder what you do. Unless the scanning being undertaken is in relation to the key priorities and concerns of senior managers, and unless it is being done in a cohesive way that leads to business outcomes, the work you produce will appear as nothing more than junk mail in their in-trays.

These are all easy traps to fall into. Early in my foresight career I felt I needed to be across everything. I thought that was my job. I read as many articles as possible, I subscribed to *The Economist* and *New Scientist*; I joined futures societies, federations and associations; I received news feeds from around the world. The result? Total data overload and office clutter. Each night my inbox would fill with emails I didn't have time to read, while the magazines just piled up, destined to remain entombed in their plastic wrapping. You soon tire of paying for subscriptions you don't use.

Environmental scanning is about research

Specifically, environmental scanning involves three types of research:

1. personal
2. historical
3. external.

1. PERSONAL RESEARCH — KNOW THYSELF

What do you think the futures could be?

Scanning starts with the scanner. While the activity of scanning is strongly associated with external insights, the process should actually begin with internal insights and becoming conscious of your own perceptions. It's these perceptions that unconsciously guide what you look for, where you look and how you interpret the information you find. Information that does not 'fit' with your personal perceptions is more likely to go unnoticed, be discarded or slip down the pecking order of importance. *Stuff that fits*, on the other hand, is likely to be given a favourable hearing and higher priority. This is just human nature.

However, effective environmental scanning is about taking an egalitarian approach to information and different perspectives. After all, 'you can't *know* what will be important ahead of time. Relevance can only be "known" a posteriori (i.e. with 20-20 hindsight)'.[3]

Such an approach to scanning requires conscious application and discipline. An effective method of ensuring such an approach is to examine and document your mindset as it relates to each scanning task:

- What do I consider to be the most likely outcomes for the issue under exploration?
- Which factors do I consider to be significant in shaping the futures of this issue?

Your responses to such questions provide an insight into your personal assumptions and expectations. By making these thoughts explicit, you arm yourself with a checklist for future reference: *Now that I'm aware of what I think, what counter-views exist?* Awareness of initial perceptions should therefore ensure a broader, more balanced scanning process and output.

I'll leave the final word on the value of personal research to Joseph Voros, my former lecturer at the Australian Foresight Institute, who has written extensively on the art of environmental scanning and the importance of the scanner's mindset[4]:

In my view, carrying out environmental scanning well is less about technique and methodology (although they are obviously important) and more about openness of mind. In fact, I would go further and claim that it is incalculably more about the *interior consciousness* of the scanner than it is about the quality of information and/or the number of sources being scanned in the exterior world.

2. HISTORICAL RESEARCH — DRIVERS OF PAST AND PRESENT PERFORMANCE

Which forces underpin historical and present-day operations and performance?

Having started the scanning process by looking within, the next step is to look to the past, or more specifically, to understand *the forces that have shaped the historical and current performance of the issue under exploration.*

This defies the natural temptation to head off into exploring the future at a hundred miles an hour. However, understanding the historical and present-day drivers of a situation provides the scanner with another invaluable framework with which to approach their task.

Taking this historical approach informs you of the original purpose of the issue, how the issue evolved into its current situation, the forces that underpinned this evolution and what drives today's operations.

Such understanding helps to detach the scanner from being wed to 'the way things are' by reinforcing the transience of dominant paradigms. Often it's hard to see past prevailing systems and behaviours, yet by taking the long view we can see that many of the mainstream activities we take for granted today have been around for only the past five minutes, figuratively speaking ('I can't do without my mobile phone!'). Also, the possibilities for future scenarios are broadened by the realisation that many so-called 'radical' ideas already existed in the past in one form or another.

The right questions, the right places

This stage of the scanning process aims to improve understanding around several key areas:

- **Where have we come from?** What was the original purpose of the issue or topic under exploration?

- **How did we get here?** What was the journey to today's dynamics and what were the forces and conditions (context) that helped to shape these outcomes?
- **How do things currently work?** What are the drivers of today's operations and performance?

The understanding that emerges from this historical research is critical to asking the *right questions* throughout the ongoing scenarios process, and also to ensuring that external research is conducted in the *right places*. It provides a platform for identifying factors that are changing or could change in the way they influence future operations and performance.

iSTEEP factors

To assist with your research, it is useful to work through a checklist of categories to ensure you get full coverage of the key historical and present-day drivers. Typically, these drivers are grouped into five broad categories—Social, Technological, Economic, Environmental and Political (STEEP). I also like to add the **Industry** category (**i**) to represent drivers in the transactional environment. Within these six categories are the drivers that have shaped the past, drivers that are shaping the present, and the factors that could shape future operations and performance:

- **Industry** factors include customers, suppliers, manufacturers, regulators, distributors, competitors, employees, unions and other industry-related stakeholders.
- **Social** factors include the *people* aspects of the system—physical and mental factors such as demographics, social values, worldviews, culture, customs, health and education.
- **Technological** factors include ongoing technology advancements (speed, size) as well as access to, use of and cost of technology.
- **Economic** factors include income and wealth, employment and industry dynamics, exchange rates, inflation, trade, energy prices, debt and interest rates.

- **Environmental** factors include the *natural* aspects of the system, such as access to natural resources, climate and other ecological factors.
- **Political** factors include the 'rules of the game'—the enablers and prohibitors that provide a structure for social and industry behaviour. These include government policies, expenditure, funding, taxes, regulations and geopolitical relations.

CASE STUDY

Australian retail landscape, 1990–2010

In 2011 I published an article titled 'Is our love affair with consumption over?'[5] This article appeared amid the enthusiastic celebration of Myer Melbourne's reopening of their flagship city shopping complex.[6] In the article I proposed that this premature celebration might have overlooked a subtle yet profound shift in consumer thinking. Because if the Australian consumer had indeed fallen out of love with consumption, then there could not have been a worse time for an organisation to spend $300 million on renovations to sell more 'stuff' to a society whose wardrobes were already 'stuffed'.

It's easy to see why the decision to undertake such a massive investment was made. For the previous two decades Australian retail had been basking in the golden age of want: an age when people's material wants were satisfied to an unprecedented level. Metaphorically, Australia had shifted from a lay-by culture of delayed gratification to a 48 months interest-free society ('I deserve this now').

With the consumer's seemingly unquenchable thirst for something more or something new, rampant materialism had become the most powerful force for retail and economic growth, and retailers and manufacturers prospered. Now, *if* the influence of this mindset was to continue, then the move to invest $300 million in refurbishing a major shopping complex made sense. But what if people's values were changing?

This is where an understanding of historical and present-day drivers is so critical to planning for the future. By explicitly outlining those factors that drive the system, historical outcomes are placed in context, and assumptions, expectations and critical uncertainties about the future become apparent.

Characteristics and drivers of the Australian retail landscape between 1990 and 2010 included:

- **industry factors**
    - business models — foot traffic, face-to-face interaction, customer service
    - customer dynamics — premiumisation of tastes, emphasis on brands
    - expansion — growth in physical number of stores
    - worldviews — *bigger is better; build it and they will come*
- **social factors**
    - demographics — growing population
    - social values — rising materialism (the *age of want*), individualism (*express yourself*), instant gratification ('I want it now!')
    - worldviews — consumption as *identity* ('I am what I own'; 'I am what I wear'), possessions as *status*, retail as *therapy*
    - culture — urbanisation, busy-ness, convenience (*time is money*)
- **technological factors**
    - absence of online competition

- **economic factors**
  - prosperity — sustained economic growth, rising household wealth
  - finance — increasing access to credit ('48 months interest free'), escalating consumer debt
  - globalisation
  - worldviews – growth is good
- **environmental factors**
  - worldviews — resources are abundant
- **political factors**
  - regulations — increased trading hours.

As you can see from this quick list of drivers and characteristics, this research phase should uncover a mix of 'hard' factors (demographic, economic, regulatory) and 'soft' factors (social values, worldviews, culture). And it's these softer elements, often forming the foundation of business performance, that tend to be ignored or taken for granted by decision makers. Worldviews and values ultimately drive attitudes and behaviours. When these significant 'softer' elements are not consciously acknowledged, managers simply assume they are the norm and will remain so into the future.

3. EXTERNAL RESEARCH — SOURCES OF FUTURE CHANGE

Which factors are changing or could change in the way they influence operations and performance?

External research looks for the fault lines that cast uncertainty over the future, cracks in the current system that loom as potential discontinuities offering both opportunities and threats. This research is intimately related to your understanding of the current system, as outlined in the previous historical research step, and to the managerial assumptions inherent in the strategic challenge.

Returning to the previous retail example, and working across the iSTEEP categories, three key drivers stand out in terms of their influence on retail operations and performance over the years 1990 to 2010:

1. **Materialism.** Retailers had been major beneficiaries of the materialism zeitgeist; in football parlance, they had been kicking with the aid of a strong breeze for the previous 20 years.

2. **Economic prosperity.** Australia had enjoyed uninterrupted economic growth since the early 1990s, providing the environment for high consumer confidence and spending.

3. **Foot traffic.** The in-store experience was seen as critical to customer loyalty. Even as late as 2010 the impact of online retail had yet to bite, and there remained genuine scepticism and uncertainty about its future impact.

For a retailer planning for the future, the risk was in assuming that these favourable drivers of past performance would simply continue. We see these assumptions in the commentary on consumption and online retailing from leading retail executives at the time. 'Consumers *will return to normal behaviour,*' insisted Paul Zahra, Chief Executive of David Jones, in 2012, 'but we need to take this time now, as painful as it is, to improve.'[7] In 2008 Gerry Harvey, Executive Chairman of Harvey Norman, declared,

> **The whole world was conned with online retailing. People say I'm a dinosaur — but it's a complete con. If you said to me in 50 years will people be successful, then yeah, but mostly not now.**[8]

The actions of Myer executives suggest that these assumptions were all too common. In adopting a scenario planning approach to strategy development, however, and particularly when weighing up the decision to invest $300 million in a store refurbishment, external research would have naturally focused on these three factors to determine:

*   the uncertainty of their future influence
*   the legitimacy of alternative sources of influence.

Like a lawyer preparing a case for uncertainty, you seek out sources and types of information that challenge or validate the legitimacy of managerial assumptions. And in 2010 these sources and types of information were there for all to see:

- Increasing concerns about climate change and the environment were well established and had played a key part in deciding the 2007 Australian federal election. These concerns hinted at the shifting public sentiment away from conspicuous consumption and towards post-materialism.
- Publications challenging rampant materialism[9] or promoting the emergence of a new type of mindset[10] were becoming more common.
- Amazon was well established as a global online trader.
- Patrick McGorry was named Australian of the Year in 2010 for his services to youth mental health, helping to raise awareness of the silent epidemic of mental health issues in society.
- Another perception pioneer was Rachel Botsman, whose ideas on collaborative consumption were beginning to gain traction: 'A power drill will be used around 12–13 minutes in its entire lifetime. It's kind of ridiculous right? Because what you need is the hole, not the drill.'[11]

There were more than enough signals in 2010, and indeed earlier, to cast doubt on the assumption that the key drivers of retail performance over the preceding 20 years would continue unchanged into the future. In the Myer example, the prospect of a decline in rampant materialism and the growth in online retail, with their potential to fundamentally change industry dynamics, should have emerged as the obvious critical uncertainties to be explored prior to undertaking their planned refurbishment.

Environmental scanning is about stimulation

One final trap to avoid when scanning is the misconception that the task is about accumulating large amounts of data. It's not about quantity. Too often I've seen environmental scans prepared ahead of scenario workshops that were just too exhaustive, as if the scanner were scanning for themselves, rather than serving the interests of the project. The predictable outcome for such efforts is that they lie unused. This is why understanding the purpose of scanning is so important.

Before developing the scenarios, the purpose of environmental scanning is twofold:

1. to identify sources of change that hold significance for the organisation's strategic challenge — those factors that could really make a difference to future outcomes within the scenario time frame
2. to stimulate and broaden the organisation's thinking about what is plausible, *what could be*, in the future.

This second purpose can be achieved only if the environmental scan is 'consumed' by its intended users. Success therefore relies on the content of the environmental scan being delivered in a format that encourages active *usage* and *digestion*. Anything less will result in a lot of wasted effort and ultimately scenarios that lack novelty. Remember, an environmental scan is useful only if it is read, considered (in terms of relevance to the strategic challenge) and shared (with fellow scenario builders), so less can sometimes be more.

To help with digestion of the scan, it's useful to remember that the contents do not necessarily have to be in a 'serious' or academic format, or in folders the size of encyclopedias. This is just another way to ensure the scan remains unused. Nothing turns down people's engagement and enthusiasm levels quicker than being confronted with the dry, dense logic of a 'formal' report. Instead, try to present even the most serious information in easily digestible formats (newspaper articles, videos, presentations, stories, graphs). Of course this may not always be possible, but a diverse mix of content formats always makes the environmental scan more interesting and user-friendly for the recipient.

The key with the scan is to remember that you're targeting the mindsets of the intended users. So always accompany scanning information with questions that prompt thinking around its relevance to the strategic challenge—'If this issue were to continue or emerge, what might it mean for our business?' In my experience, the questions you pose in the environmental scan are as important as the information itself. As Marcus Barber once told me, 'An effective environmental scan can identify both existing and new information to the reader, but always strives to bring new relevance.'

CHAPTER 10

'What's next?' — Anticipating the future

Scenarios provide the essential creativity for strategic transformation

Conditioned by a culture of evidence-based (after-the-fact) decision making, it's not hard to see why some people can struggle initially with creating scenarios. Time and again I've seen how participants can hit a wall at this stage of the strategy process. People who comfortably embraced each of the previous stages — internal interviews, environmental scanning, sorting of uncertainties and choosing driving forces — suddenly freeze at the prospect of imagining circumstances that don't yet exist, frozen by a combination of insecurity (*What if I'm wrong?*), uncertainty (*This could happen or that could happen*), lack of creative belief (*How would I know?*) or the absence of supporting data (*Where are the facts?*).

It's this absence of facts, the scaffolding for their everyday decision making, and the pivot to relying on intuition, creativity and logic, that usually proves most challenging to scenario builders.

Does it make sense?

This chapter describes the *intuitive logics* approach to creating scenarios that was developed by Royal Dutch Shell and SRI International during the 1970s.[1] In lay terms, this technique applies a 'Does it make sense?' approach to exploring the future based on the logic of *cause* (drivers) and *effect* (outcomes) relationships.

Intuitive logics is primarily a qualitative technique, with secondary quantitative support. Such an approach, with its emphasis on participant creativity, recognises the non-linear development of the future.

Some people initially struggle with this approach; I should know, because I was one of them.

Letting go of command and control

Coming out of a business training background that was heavily focused on data and trend analysis, my initial impression of the intuitive logics approach was that it was just too 'loose'. Where were the facts? Where was the structure? The process was so far removed from my perceptions around 'serious information' that it was hard to imagine anything worthwhile coming from the exercise.

My response to this perceived lack of structure was to go too far the other way. I tried to introduce a rigorous process at Foster's that would bring discipline to our scenario building. In doing so, I served only to stifle creativity—the essence of successful scenario generation.

My innovation was a 'Futures Grid', a massive spreadsheet in which I attempted to cover every imaginable outcome of the future. Down the side axis were the two scenario drivers as well as up to eight other significant influencing factors identified by the participants. Along the top axis were topics and questions for participants to consider in developing their scenario relating to work, education, media, public services, even social epidemics and so on. In all, 19 dimensions across and 10 down. I was actually asking participants to consider and discuss 190 variables and their possible outcomes. And that was just the first iteration!

Initially, at least, I thought I was on a winner. I even wrote an essay on the process in the second year of my master's studies (it received a generous C grade). In fact, this is a model of what *not* to do. My thinking reflected a poor understanding of both the purpose and the process of scenarios. Such a detailed and regimented approach is a creativity killer. Just as important, it kills the fun of building scenarios. It replaces collaborative creativity with arduous task-mastering.

Inherent in this approach was my 'command and control' mindset, a belief that if I just asked enough questions about enough variables then I would get the future *right*. For example, I was even asking people to consider how the future of Steiner schools could be affected in their scenarios!

I quickly realised that this intensive and rigid approach wasn't the answer either.

Bringing everyone along

Perhaps the most underrated element of the scenarios process is workshop design and facilitation. In the design, it's important to acknowledge that participants will have varying degrees of experience with creating scenarios and different expectations about what is to follow. At the start of every workshop I ask people to raise their hand if they've done scenarios before, and the response is always the same. A few people raise their hands hesitantly and then share their experiences rather vaguely: 'We did something similar at a place I used to work' or 'The work we did was more like forecasts or computer simulations'. These responses go to the heart of one of the issues identified in chapter 2: scenarios remain a fuzzy concept.

The fact is, actual experience with the intuitive logics method is not that common, so almost everyone in the room will be about to enter new territory, where they'll create strategy in a quite different way.

Adding to this challenge will be the natural uncertainty people feel with regard to planning for the longer term. It's easy to forget how overwhelming it can be to think about what could happen over the next 5, 10 or 20 years. Most people in the room probably haven't confirmed their plans for the coming weekend. This is where I find the words of Herman Kahn can be useful to relax people: 'Remember, it's only a scenario.' We're not trying to predict the future, we're trying to learn from it so we can improve our decision making. This is no different from the scenario drills sporting teams practise every week at training.

For a facilitator, appreciating the lack of scenario experience and the feelings of doubt among attendees is critical. It places an emphasis on bringing everyone along at the same pace and not losing anyone along the way.

Stimulation and structure

It's the pivot from understanding the present to envisioning the future that always proves most difficult for scenario participants. Suddenly people are no longer thinking or talking about the things they know, or the things they can see or touch (behaviours and infrastructure, for example). Instead, they're being asked to think of things that don't physically exist, to consider changes that *might* occur. Again, for most participants it's likely to be the first time they've ever undertaken such an activity.

Successful scenario building relies on stimulation and structure to break down the complexity of the future: *stimulation* to ensure participants always have the resources (the prospective armoury) to call upon to envisage future developments; and *structure* to ensure logical flow, a process in which each step builds on the last and in turn provides input into subsequent activities.

As this stimulation and structure take effect, anxiety and uncertainty give way to the sound of robust discussion as participants relax into the exercise and enthusiastically embrace being part of something different—'I get this. I know why we're doing this activity and I know where we're headed'. This participant buy-in, understanding and enthusiasm are the essential foundation for successful scenario planning.

CASE STUDY

Melton City Council, 2017–18

Melton City Council is the local governing body for the City of Melton, one of the fastest-growing regions in the western suburbs of Melbourne, Victoria. Driven by a mix of young families and immigration, the population has soared from approximately 50 000 people in the year 2000 to its present number of 150 000. Numbers are expected to double again over coming decades, and a population of approximately 400 000 is expected by 2050.

Such growth places enormous pressures on planning for community infrastructure and services. It also presents challenges for internal planning to ensure Council has the resources and capabilities to deliver on community expectations.

Internal planning

To meet these challenges, Council decided to design a long-term corporate strategy and a shorter-term implementation plan around the following strategic challenge:

What will our organisation look like in 2036 as it delivers on Melton City 2036: The City We Imagine?

The horizon year of 2036 was chosen to ensure that the corporate strategy aligned with the community's vision for the future, which had previously been shared in the document *Melton City 2036: The City We Imagine*. The wording of the strategic challenge explicitly linked Council's future success to its capacity to deliver on the community's vision.

Three key objectives for the project were agreed:

1. Describe Council's desired state at 2036 and an action plan to achieve it. *What* is Council doing, *how* is it doing it, and *what* capabilities, resources and processes are required to deliver the necessary services and infrastructure for our community?
2. Set out the *mission*, *vision* and *priorities* for Council as a business.
3. Provide direction and a framework for cohesive and timely planning and decision making across the organisation.

Given the length of the planning horizon and its associated uncertainty, scenarios sat at the heart of this project. Future scenarios would be developed to explore the different environments in which Council might have to operate, thus providing the *why* for Council's response to the strategic challenge.

This project effectively involved three phases: building scenarios for 2036, designing a long-term corporate strategy, and developing a shorter-term implementation plan to support the corporate strategy. Managerial support for the project was unanimous and participation in all phases would involve the CEO, his three general managers and all 17 managers, representing Council's entire leadership team. The project was sponsored by a working group of six managers, and an internal coordinator was responsible for day-to-day management. This coordinator would also be responsible for ongoing reporting on progress of the eventual implementation plan, completing the loop in a world-class, end-to-end strategy process.

This case study describes *phase one* of this project; the creation of four scenarios in a workshop setting to enable leaders at Melton City Council to address the strategic challenge, *What will our organisation look like in 2036?*

Workshop priming

Leading into the two-day scenarios workshop, participants received three sets of stimuli to ensure they arrived with clear expectations about what was to unfold and inspired imaginations about what could be (see figure 10.1, overleaf). The first of these was a briefing presentation I was asked to deliver three weeks before the workshop. Such a briefing had never been part of my process before, but I recognised the potential benefits; as the workshop approached, a slight sense of managerial anxiety needed to be placated. This is something you come across time and time again, and again it's the mysterious black box that is scenarios that's the cause. *How do we keep the scenarios from being too fantastical? What information will we receive to help us think about the next two decades? When do we get this information?*

I cannot overstate how much this session contributed towards what became a very successful two days of scenario building. The purpose of the upcoming workshop (where it sat within the overall project), the process (pre-reads, workshop activities) and expectations (outcomes and next steps) were all outlined and received with greater clarity than any email could have hoped to achieve. As a result, feelings of apprehension, doubt or uncertainty now gave way to enthusiasm, understanding and confidence.

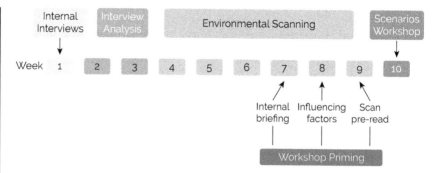

Figure 10.1: workshop priming

Timely and effective workshop priming ensures participants are mentally and emotionally prepared for their futures journey.

Two weeks out from the workshop, attendees received pre-work asking them to consider factors in the *external environment* that could influence outcomes and responses to the strategic challenge. To help identify these influencing factors, participants were asked to consider the same questions I had used for environmental scanning:

- Which factors underpin current and historical Melton City Council operations or performance?
- Which factors are changing or could change in the way they influence Melton City Council operations or performance?

Participants were asked to complete a template (see table 10.1) listing up to three factors in each of the iSTEEP categories that they felt could have a significant influence on the future operations of Council (what they're doing and how they're doing it). Where possible, and if appropriate, they were encouraged to use language that captured the uncertain future impact of the factor, acknowledging the ambiguity associated with long-term change (*the extent or degree to which ..., the impact or level of ...* and so on).[2]

Recipients were then asked to return their completed templates one week before the workshop and to bring a copy to the workshop.

Table 10.1: which external factors could influence responses to the strategic challenge: 'What will our organisation look like in 2036 as it delivers on *Melton City 2036: The City We Imagine?*'

Industry	Degree to which state government pursues further council amalgamations	Degree to which rate-capping affects Council's capacity to deliver services	Impact of potential changes in direction from new Councils every 4 years
Social	Impact of changing levels of community trust in government	Level of future population growth	Impact of generational differences and expectations on employment practices
Technological	Extent to which customer expectations for service are driven by technology	Extent to which technology can deliver appropriate efficiencies	Impact of technology on communities of interest vs neighbourhood communities
Economic	Impact of changes in manufacturing on local employment options	Impact of interest rates on home owners and home ownership	Level of Australian engagement in overseas conflicts and impact on budget spend
Environmental	Impact of food scarcity and/or food security on community behaviour	Impact of water availability on local environment	Impact of improvements in recycling practices
Political	Impact of potential future urban growth boundary changes	Impact of gaining or losing other government funding avenues	Extent to which future immigration levels change

The quality of pre-workshop thinking, demonstrated in the output above, guaranteed attendees arrived with the necessary prospective armoury for a successful scenarios workshop.

This pre-work activity is significant for a couple of reasons:

1. It meets the stimulation criteria, ensuring attendees arrive with the necessary prospective armoury in their minds. This is evident in the richness of the responses shown in table 10.1. Any scenarios exercise in which attendees put this quality of thought into the strategic challenge before the workshop is almost guaranteed to get off to a great start.

2. By asking for the pre-work to be submitted prior to the workshop, the facilitator gets a head start, gaining a further sense of the issues at the top of people's minds and of the themes likely to emerge during the workshop. In the context of a time-constrained workshop, such preparation can be priceless.

Finally, one week before the workshop attendees received the environmental scan as a pre-read. As much as anything, an effective environmental scan can smash pre-existing perceptions about what constitutes 'useful' information. Heading into a workshop to explore the next two decades, people will naturally expect a folder full of tables, charts, forecasts and trends. Good luck getting people to read that. Instead, the 21 leaders received a scan with links to 66 articles of interest. Each attendee was allocated three articles as their pre-read, and a further three articles were allocated to everyone. Each article was accompanied by several questions prompting consideration of future impact and uncertainty.

The novelty of this approach—providing digestible hints about what *could* happen, rather than detailed prescriptions of what *will* happen (forecasts, trends)—is both energising and empowering. It reinforces for attendees that the future is uncertain and that the output of the upcoming workshop will be based on *their* intuition, insights and judgement.

Scenarios workshop

Building scenarios is best done within diverse teams, where the variety of experience, knowledge, and opinion optimises the prospects for useful strategic insights. Participants in the Melton City Council scenarios worked within teams of five and six people. These numbers were ideal as experience has shown that having more than four people in a group is essential for a range of views, yet having more than seven can make it too easy for people to take a back seat, or to get lost in the noise, and hence leave their opinions stifled.

Diversity of opinion is important because it can prevent the kind of groupthink that develops when people of similar values and experience get together to create scenarios. When we first embarked on our scenarios journey at Foster's, we decided to explore the long-term future of the Australian beer market. These scenarios were created entirely by internal employees, predominantly working across innovation and marketing, and aged in their twenties and thirties. One of the scenarios described an increasingly polarised world of 'haves' and 'have nots', a society of gated communities and restricted events that minimised interaction between different segments of the community. It was during this exercise that I overheard one of the more remarkable comments in my time building scenarios. In describing the scenario to me, one of the participants said, 'This is the type of world where people get a weekly massage', then after a pause he mused, 'But I suppose most people already do that today, don't they?'

The participatory team approach to scenario building works well because creating scenarios is a democratic process. After all, if there are no facts about the long-term future, then there can be no experts. So, regardless of industry experience or managerial seniority, everyone pretty much starts from the same place, and all opinions should be treated as equally valid. In fact, in my experience it's often the more senior managers, with their paradigm expertise, who can find it hardest to imagine future alternatives.

HOW MANY SCENARIOS?

The following process describes my preferred approach to building scenarios, applying the intuitive logics technique to create four scenarios using the 2 × 2 matrix method. This method, which has proven an effective and popular form of scenario building, involves choosing two scenario drivers based on their perceived level of future uncertainty and potential to have an impact on responses to the strategic challenge. Axes are then determined for each uncertainty by creating spectrums of plausible outcomes (e.g. high/low), giving you a matrix of four different quadrants in which to build scenarios.

Over the years I have also experimented with creating both three and two scenarios and have found that these approaches can also be effective. Now, many texts warn of the dangers in producing three scenarios, with managers likely to think of them in terms of a good, bad and on-trend forecast, then showing their preference for the perceived safety of the middle ground. This was never my experience. Scenarios should never be presented or interpreted as good, bad or otherwise. All scenarios should be neutral and equally plausible.

We employed the three scenarios approach for a Foster's project looking at the impact of an ageing population on the future of alcohol consumption. In this project, three scenarios were created around the uncertain influence of one particular driver—social values. Accordingly, scenarios were created to reflect the different influence traditionalist, materialist and post-materialist values might have on the future attitudes, lifestyles and choices of baby boomers.

Two scenarios were developed for the successful State Library of Victoria project in 2012 looking at the strategic challenge, 'What is a public library in 2030' (discussed in chapter 11). In this project, the choice of two scenarios had much to do with the complexity of managing the input of 80 participants. The successful outcomes of this project, evident in the transformational strategic recommendations and subsequent implementation, prove that two scenarios can be just as effective as four in generating a positive strategic impact.

My preference for four scenarios is based on past experience where, in a participatory setting, inexperienced practitioners have found it easier to develop scenarios when they have a combination of driving forces to provide the logic of their world. Two forces interacting can provide greater scope and structure for scenario builders when using the 2 x 2 matrix approach. Creating four scenarios does increase the complexity for drawing strategic conclusions; however, it also provides you with greater coverage of plausible future outcomes without going overboard (to six, eight or ten scenarios, say).

SCENARIO EQUALITY

The creativity challenge in scenario building is to develop futures that are equally plausible and equally useful for managers to respond to. In developing scenarios, it's only natural that people will have a preference for one particular future over another. We prefer the scenario that more closely 'matches' our personal view of the future (the 'right' scenario). We prefer the scenario in which our company prospers by continuing to do what it does (the 'good' scenario) or the scenario in which we would like to live (the 'utopian' scenario).

On the other hand, you're bound to come across participants who don't build their scenarios with the same level of enthusiasm. In these instances, the process can become a grind as you hear comments like 'We don't like our world', 'We want to choose different drivers' or 'This scenario is no good for our company'. Worse still are people who simply refuse to engage with the scenario because it doesn't match their expectations of the future ('This is just fantasy').

The future is likely to reflect a blend of scenarios, rather than a single one. Accordingly, each scenario should be treated as part of a set, in which one weak link can diminish their overall usefulness. Treating each scenario as a piece of the future, you want as complete a picture as possible to inform your thinking. Hence, the emphasis must be on treating the process as an exercise in creativity, in which the challenge is to develop plausible and strategically useful futures.

Workshop process

The workshop process has five phases:

1. Reviewing the environmental scan
2. Identifying influencing factors
3. Sorting and prioritising influencing factors
4. Choosing scenario drivers
5. Building scenarios.

1. Reviewing the environmental scan

In the previous chapter I wrote that the only useful environmental scan is one that is read, considered and shared. The best way to achieve this outcome is by introducing accountability, not in a disciplinary or authoritarian sense, but through an engaging and interactive exercise that enthuses people to think, *I can't wait to share this.*

I begin each scenarios workshop with a group activity in which each attendee presents their allocated pre-work, offers their personal thoughts on relevance to the strategic challenge, then invites others to share their views. As a scenario activity, this exercise is the equivalent of stretching before a big race, mentally limbering up as a way of easing participants into the future.

What follows should be a vibrant and engaging session that ensures the significant contents and implications of the environmental scan are processed by the members of each group, and that participants are stimulated to consider implications and opportunities in terms of the strategic challenge. You know an environmental scan is effective when participants find themselves referring back to its contents and implications time and again throughout the workshop.

2. Identifying influencing factors

Building scenarios begins with identifying and understanding influencing factors—those factors in the external environment that could influence future outcomes and affect responses to the strategic challenge. Because they are external to the organisation, influencing factors sit outside your direct control in either the transactional or the contextual environment ('external cause / internal effect'[3]).

Calling upon their earlier pre-work (see table 10.1 for an example) and using the environmental scan as further stimulus, participants share their thoughts on which factors could influence outcomes and responses to the strategic challenge. This exercise works best when conducted in the following way:

1. Each person reviews the list of influencing factors from their pre-work and chooses three factors they feel could have greatest influence in shaping outcomes and responses to the strategic challenge—*what could really make a difference?*

2. Working around the group, each person nominates one of their chosen influencing factors and puts forward their reasoning for why it is significant. What follows should be an extended period of group discussion as members share and capture their thoughts on why each factor is significant.

Questions to consider during this stage should cover change, impact and uncertainty:

1. **What do we know about this factor?** What is changing? What's the status of this issue? What was in the environmental scan?

2. **Why is this factor significant?** How could it affect us? This is where the relevance and implications to the strategic challenge should be made explicit.

3. **What does this factor rely on?** How uncertain is future development? Which other forces could influence this factor?

This process continues until each person has exhausted their three chosen factors (if one has already been chosen by another person, choose an alternative).

Each group typically emerges from this stage with a list of 10–20 influencing factors and a template of material relating to each. A sample from the Melton City Council workshop appears in table 10.2, showing the type and quality of output generated during this stage.

Table 10.2: building scenarios starts with identifying factors that could influence responses to the strategic challenge, 'What will our organisation look like as it delivers on Melton City 2036?'

	What do we know about this factor? What is changing?	Why is this factor significant? How could it affect us?
Influencing factor: Impact of minor political parties and Independents	The vote for major parties is declining. There is an increasing number of micro, single issue and niche parties. We are closer to having hung parliaments with less decisive majorities. Distrust of politics, politicians, political systems, political machinery is rising. Individualism is rising.	It compromises political direction/decision making/implementation of policy. It becomes more complex in determining who we should interact with, which changes the way advocacy looks. Political instability means we're always on the verge of an election. It impacts Council's long-term planning, creating uncertainty.

Group discussion about the significant influencing factors should lead to shared understanding and greater clarity about what really matters in relation to the strategic challenge.

LABELLING INFLUENCING FACTORS

I mentioned earlier how we undertook a scenario planning project at Foster's looking at the future of Australia's ageing population and its potential impact on the domestic alcohol market. On day one of a three-day workshop, participants working in groups discussed and then listed those factors they felt could have greatest significance for the strategic challenge. A sample of these factors appears in figure 10.2.

This example, with its vague labels, topics and actions, is typical of scenario exercises involving inexperienced participants, and the contrast with the previous output in table 10.2 from the same stage of the Melton City Council workshop is stark.

Figure 10.2: factors influencing baby boomers and alcohol consumption

Influencing factors that are presented as vague topics, or misrepresented as inevitable trends, leave participants with a shortage of mental stimulation as they begin the scenario building process.

In figure 10.2 we see many examples of the types of errors commonly made by scenario novices:

- **Factors are described as actions.** Actions are responses, not drivers of future context ('protect environment through sustainable practices','government legislates against boomer excesses').
- **Factor descriptions are vague** ('employment flexibility', 'single-person households','need for protection'). How can you make sense of what was intended?
- **Factors are directional.** Directional language ignores future uncertainty and assumes the future development of a factor is predetermined ('rise of post-materialism';'boomers continue to drive political agenda').

From such a vague platform, it's little wonder that participants find the pivot to scenario building such a challenge; you're sending people off into the future with inadequate mental stimulation and understanding.

Influencing factors 'should be expressed in as few words as possible, but sufficient to make them understandable to everyone'.[4] It's important to remember a few simple guidelines here:

- Avoid labels that are too broad or vague ('social values', 'population','interest rates').
- Where an outcome is uncertain, avoid using language that implies predetermined direction—that is, precludes movement in another direction ('rise of far-right politics', 'rising cost of living').
- Uncertain factors should be expressed using neutral language that captures their future ambiguity. Such language acknowledges that future developments could go one way or the other, allowing for the spectrum of movement on which scenario building is based ('extent to which social values evolve').

Variations on this sort of language might include:

- — '*impact of* autonomous vehicles on lifestyles and infrastructure'
- — '*degree to which* traffic congestion affects desire to live in large cities'
- — '*level of* agreement between political parties on climate change'
- — '*changing attitudes* to minor parties and independent political candidates'.

• Directional language should be used only where the outcome is relatively predetermined and there is limited scope for future variability ('impact of an ageing population').

3. Sorting and prioritising influencing factors

Sorting and prioritising influencing factors can be a stumbling block for even the most experienced scenario planner. Fundamentally, the task at this stage is to bring a sense of order to the previous output by categorising each influencing factor according to perceived impact (on the strategic challenge) and perceived uncertainty (in terms of future development).

I've found it's not so much that the task is difficult, but rather that the terminology used to describe the activity's purpose and process can sometimes cause confusion for participants. Language and clarity of meaning are critical during this activity.

It can be useful to begin this step by revisiting the purpose of scenario planning; scenarios provide plausible future contexts to rehearse decision making and inform strategy development. They do not have to be distinct, but they must be significantly different so as to evoke different strategic responses from decision makers. At the heart of the scenario process is the acknowledgement that the future is uncertain and we are therefore planning for uncertainty.

The purpose of this step is to isolate those influencing factors that are most significant for the strategic challenge and also highly uncertain in terms of how they could develop. It's this range of uncertainty that pulls your scenarios apart, providing the divergent logics of your scenario axes. The two factors agreed to be most impactful and uncertain are then chosen as the driving forces to shape your scenario developments and outcomes (see figure 10.3).

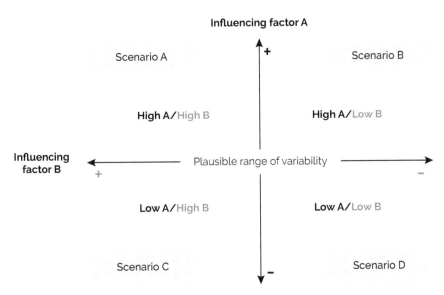

Figure 10.3: 2 × 2 scenario matrix

The scenario logics in a 2 × 2 matrix are 'pulled apart' by the range of variability of your two scenario drivers, prompting different responses to the strategic challenge in each scenario.

IMPACT/UNCERTAINTY MATRIX

Use of an impact/uncertainty matrix to sort and prioritise influencing factors is a well-established step in the scenario building process. Essentially, this involves categorising the influencing factors according to their relative impact and uncertainty (low, medium or high) in order to isolate those factors which are high impact/high uncertainty:

- **high impact**

  significance—would really make a difference to how you respond to the strategic challenge

- **high uncertainty**

  variability—range of plausible future outcomes (could go one way or the other).

Each group then plot their influencing factors on individual matrices according to their relative significance and uncertainty. Since the purpose of this activity is to isolate *what really matters* in relation to the strategic challenge and to planning for an uncertain future, and because this is an exercise in relativity, no more than 25 per cent of factors should appear in the high impact / high uncertainty domain[5] (see figure 10.4).

ASSESSING IMPACT AND UNCERTAINTY

When assessing the impact of an influencing factor, we are interested in its relevance and significance to the strategic challenge—does this factor *really make a difference* to our responses to the strategic challenge? In making this assessment the question to ask is:

To what degree could this factor affect outcomes or responses to the strategic challenge?

It is important to assess the impact of an influencing factor first to establish relevance to the strategic challenge before discussing whether or not its future development is uncertain.[6]

As an example, let's look at the Melton City Council scenarios and the influencing factor 'Extent to which population changes'. Council management rated this factor as highly impactful given it will affect the type, location and demand for service delivery and infrastructure, and thereby influence the capabilities, resources and processes Council as an organisation will require. So this factor was initially plotted as shown on the matrix in figure 10.5.

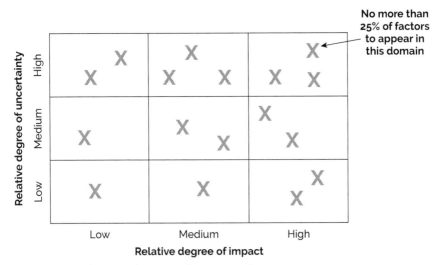

Figure 10.4: impact/uncertainty matrix

The impact/uncertainty matrix is a relatively simple yet extremely effective tool for ordering and prioritising your influencing factors.

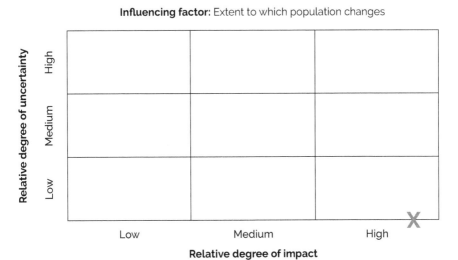

Figure 10.5: assessing the relative degree of impact

The influencing factor 'Extent to which population changes' was assessed as high impact for its potential to influence future Council capabilities, resources and processes.

Assessing the future uncertainty of an influencing factor can be trickier, and it's the language that sometimes confuses people. When we hear the words *certain* or *uncertain* in relation to the future we naturally think in terms of our own views on probability or likelihood ('I'm pretty sure this will happen' or 'I don't think that will happen'). Misunderstanding of 'uncertainty' can sometimes lead to an overrepresentation of factors in the low uncertainty domains of the matrix.

With the impact/uncertainty matrix we are interested in uncertainty as it relates to the plausible range of future development for an influencing factor—its spectrum of potential variability ('It could develop one way, or it could go another'). And in assessing whether or not the uncertainty is relatively low, medium or high we are interested in whether the range of plausible future outcomes is broad enough to provoke different responses to the strategic challenge—*does the difference make a difference*:

Is the range of plausible future variability enough to demand different strategic responses?

Returning to the influencing factor 'Extent to which population changes', we are interested in the plausible range of change when we assess its uncertainty. For instance, if the potential range of variability is agreed to be relatively insignificant, then we can say there is relative low uncertainty around this factor (see figure 10.6):

Extent to which population changes – relative certainty
Plausible range of variability +130 000 residents ⟷ +150 000 residents

In this example, the agreed range of plausible variability (20 000 residents) is *not* enough to warrant a different response to the strategic challenge, so we can plan around this factor with relative certainty.

DETERMINING UNCERTAINTY

To understand the range of plausible outcomes or future uncertainty, it is useful to consider what each factor relies on:

- What could influence future outcomes for this factor?
- How variable is the potential influence of these other factors?

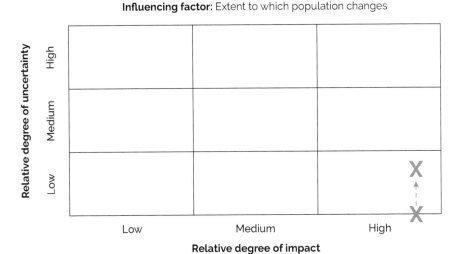

Influencing factor: Extent to which population changes

Figure 10.6: assessing the relative degree of uncertainty — low uncertainty

If the range of plausible variability is not enough to warrant different responses to the strategic challenge, then we can plan for this influencing factor with relative certainty.

By considering the plausible influences on each factor, the range of future variability should naturally extend. 'If this happened, and this happened, or this happened, I can see how our influencing factor could develop in a different direction.'

Regarding the 'Extent to which population changes', the following factors could influence future outcomes:

- rate of immigration
- appeal of Melbourne as a liveable city
- housing affordability compared with other regions/states
- safety perceptions of Melton
- preference for higher-density vs lower-density living
- appeal of regional living vs urban living.

Accordingly, a case could be made for a strategically significant variance in future population change:

Extent to which population changes – relative uncertainty
Plausible range of variability +60 000 residents ←→ +150 000 residents

In this case, the range of plausible change (90 000 residents) *is* enough to warrant a different strategic response, so we can assess this factor as highly uncertain, which it ultimately was (see figure 10.7).

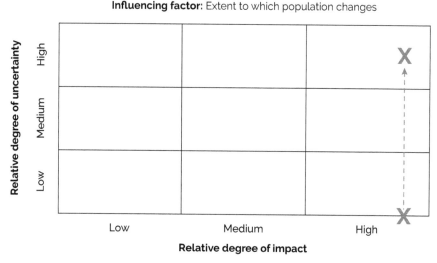

Influencing factor: Extent to which population changes

Figure 10.7: assessing the relative degree of uncertainty—high uncertainty

Where the range of plausible variability is agreed to be strategically significant, we assess the influencing factor as highly uncertain.

TRANSITIONING FROM INFLUENCING FACTORS TO DRIVING FORCES

The impact/uncertainty matrix plays the critical linking role between your influencing factors and your scenarios. The work of Ian Wilson improves the usefulness of this tool by introducing terms that explicitly link domains on the matrix to scenario development and strategic planning.[7] From a scenario development perspective, we are interested in influencing factors that appear in the shaded areas of the matrix that follows (see figure 10.8).

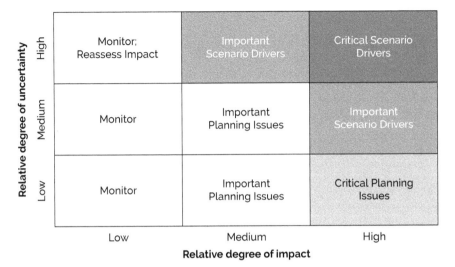

Figure 10.8: linking the impact/uncertainty matrix to scenario development

Domain names make the link between the impact/uncertainty matrix and scenario building explicit.

Critical scenario drivers are those influencing factors considered high impact and highly uncertain. The combination of these drivers provides the overarching logic and direction that weaves through your scenarios.

Influencing factors that are considered *important scenario drivers* are not discarded in the scenario process. In fact, they appear in all scenarios where they are relevant, and their uncertain future outcomes are resolved according to the logic of each scenario. For example, the uncertain influencing factor 'Extent to which population changes' could logically see growth of 60 000 residents in one scenario, yet see growth of 150 000 residents according to the equally plausible logic of another scenario.

Critical planning issues are considered to be highly impactful and to have a low potential for future variability. These are factors for which managers can plan with confidence ('This is happening — we need to be planning for this now!'). As an example, consider the influencing factor 'Impact of an ageing population'. In 2018 we can confidently plan for an ageing population because we know within a small degree of variation just how many 70-plus-year-olds there will be in 2028 — their number is already *in the pipeline* coming through.[8] Critical planning issues should be addressed in all scenarios, once again according to the overarching logic of each scenario.

Scenarios effectively describe plausible future events and outcomes representing the combined influence of these critical scenario drivers, important scenario drivers and critical planning issues, as summarised in figure 10.9 (overleaf).

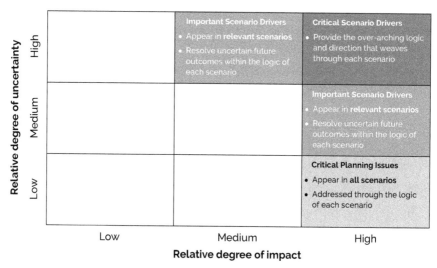

Figure 10.9: scenario building blocks

The role of each influencing factor in the scenario building process is made obvious in this impact/uncertainty matrix.

4. Choosing scenario drivers

Like the motive in a murder mystery, your critical scenario drivers provide the overarching logic and direction that weaves through each scenario. They are the key variables in the entire exercise. So it's no surprise that selecting your two scenario drivers can be the most contentious step in the scenario process. The subjectivity of the exercise naturally means participants will have different views on which variables are most important and most uncertain. And this is fine.

I mentioned earlier my scenarios project exploring the question 'What is a public library in 2030?' (This case study is discussed in depth in chapter 11.) One of the critical scenario drivers chosen in this exercise was *the increasing irrelevance and distrust of traditional gatekeepers*. Now, keep in mind that this was in June 2012; the rise of Donald Trump and the successful Brexit campaign were still years away. Personally, I doubted the value of this driver, struggling to see how it could play a significant role in shaping the future of public libraries. How wrong was I? The subsequent scenario showed how growing distrust of traditional gatekeepers could be linked to an increasing desire for community belonging and an expanded role for public libraries in facilitating this sense of belonging.

Subsequent events have not only confirmed how foresightful this choice was, but also demonstrated to me how important flexibility of perspective is at this stage of the scenario process. After all, we're talking about the future, and the future is uncertain; only 20/20 hindsight can be a true judge of what really matters. This is a point worth reiterating to participants.

By this stage of the workshop, participants should have a clear understanding of the process and appreciate that no matter which critical scenario drivers are chosen, no important influencing factor gets left behind. Still, it's important to have a process to navigate successfully around what can sometimes become an uneasy impasse.

The first step is to bring participants back to the strategic challenge, reminding them that they are assessing each potential driver on two criteria:

- **impact.** Would this factor really make a difference to how we respond to the strategic challenge?
- **uncertainty.** Is the potential for future variability enough to warrant different responses to the strategic challenge?

The two factors that are then chosen as the most impactful and the most uncertain become the critical scenario drivers.

The second step is to continue the democratic theme of the workshop. The stage of choosing scenario drivers is the first time in the workshop that individual teams come together as one to review their work, so it's important to establish a level of shared understanding. Thus, each group presents their critical scenario drivers to the broader workshop, making the case for why they consider these factors to be most impactful and most uncertain in relation to the strategic challenge.

With each team likely to present two or three scenario drivers from their impact/uncertainty matrix, there can be as many as eight or twelve factors to choose from. So it can be useful to cluster any similar drivers, and to give the new grouping an overarching label. This move should reduce the number of potential drivers to a more manageable number.

Following these presentations, an open-forum discussion should take place in which everyone is invited to contribute their views or to seek further clarity on any of the drivers presented. What follows should be a robust and lengthy discussion. For the facilitator, patience is key at this stage; it's important to allocate the necessary time to allow everyone to have their say.

At the conclusion of this discussion, each attendee is allocated two votes to choose the drivers they feel are most impactful and most uncertain. The factors with the highest number of votes then become the critical scenario drivers, with one caveat: the two drivers must be able to logically coexist. That is, in all four scenario quadrants, the impact of one driver can't preclude that of the other driver.

Melton City Council's leadership team generated a total of 36 factors that they felt could influence outcomes and responses to their strategic challenge, eight of which had been assessed by the respective scenario teams as high impact and highly uncertain:

- extent to which demand for infrastructure and service delivery changes
- level of economic performance

- degree of state government control over local government
- rate of population growth
- extent to which service delivery models change
- impact of the successor to social media on social cohesion
- degree to which council's workforce changes
- extent to which population changes.

It was during the open discussion on these critical scenario drivers that the focus on workshop stimulation and structure, and the investment in bringing everyone along, hit pay dirt. Following the respective team presentations, the leadership group enthusiastically but respectfully engaged in the process of debating the pros and cons of each critical scenario driver put forward. An hour later the group remained determined to achieve a resolution before calling it a day, fully aware of the importance of what they were trying to achieve in the context of developing scenarios. Their persistence was the ultimate symbol of process engagement and understanding.

Eventually, votes were cast and the two factors considered most important and most uncertain were:

- level of economic performance
- degree of state government control over local government.

These factors provided the following spectrums of variability to form our scenarios axes:

Level of economic performance
low-performing economy ←→ high-performing economy

Level of local government autonomy
low local government autonomy ←→ high local government autonomy

We now had the framework for what would ultimately yield four scenarios for 2036: Silicon Valley, Switzerland, MacGyver and Skyhooks (see figure 10.10, overleaf).

In the final step of the workshop process, 'Building scenarios', I describe in detail how these futures were created, using the MacGyver scenario to illustrate the evolving composition of a scenario.

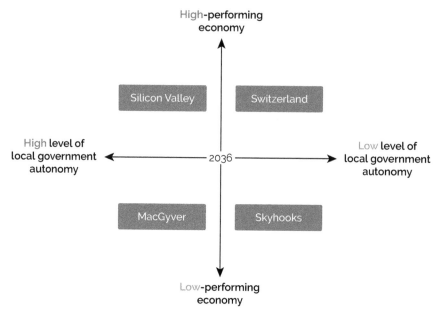

Figure 10.10: Melton City Council scenarios framework

Melton City Council's leadership team selected 'Level of economic performance' and 'Degree of state government control over local government' as their two critical scenario drivers.

MELTON CITY COUNCIL SCENARIOS FOR 2036

Here is a summary of the four MCC scenarios.

Silicon Valley

Critical scenario drivers:

- *high* economic performance
- *high* local government autonomy

Synopsis:

This scenario represents Australia's successful transition to a creative, innovative and entrepreneurial twenty-first-century economy. It's a *high-tech* scenario featuring dynamic start-up ecosystems that promote collaborative entrepreneurialism and facilitate *high social density lifestyles*. It's a scenario defined by two significant cultural transformations:

- Transforming to embrace an innovation culture; becoming a society in which education, creativity, diversity, agility and learning are celebrated, rather than one that sneers at 'inner-city latte sippers'
- Transforming to develop an entrepreneurial culture, a willingness to 'have a go', to collaborate and to 'play' with ideas.

If this scenario were a region it would be Silicon Valley; a dynamic hub bustling with large high-tech corporations and hundreds of start-up companies.

Switzerland

Critical scenario drivers:

- *high* economic performance
- *low* local government autonomy

Synopsis:

This scenario is about the *transfer of agency*:

- *from* government directive *to* personal agency ('I want what I want')
- *from* representative democracy *to* participatory agency ('I want to have a say')
- *from* short-term focus *to* future generational agency ('I want to act sustainably').

It describes the *continuing transfer of autonomy from government providers to individuals*. In doing so, it articulates how technology can be used to enable participatory democratic behaviours that produce a paradigm shift in the way community services and infrastructure are administered.

This scenario describes a wealthy, participatory democracy that is environmentally conscious, has public policies promoting greater income equality, and has a population that values personal choice and self-expression.

MacGyver

Critical scenario drivers:

- *low* economic performance
- *high* local government autonomy

Synopsis:

This scenario is defined by *community resourcefulness, self-sufficiency* and *ingenuity*. It's a response to lower economic growth, which forces people and communities to look inwards for opportunities and to become more resourceful.

Facing external constraints, people look to each other to develop innovative and efficient communal solutions to extract the value from the services and infrastructure they want. Emerging from this scenario is a *natural optimism* and willingness to work together towards sustainable, communal solutions.

This scenario is about making the most of what you have. It is defined by resourcefulness, agility, innovation and a knack for unconventional problem solving.

Skyhooks

Critical scenario drivers:

- *low* economic performance
- *low* local government autonomy

Synopsis:

This scenario is about the 'forgotten people'. It describes the effects of an economic downturn on those people most vulnerable to the world's changing economic dynamics. It depicts a future in which Australia occupies a less than competitive position in the world, having failed to address its key economic vulnerabilities, namely preparing the economy for a twenty-first-century landscape dominated by globalisation and technological changes.

Finding itself structurally ill-equipped, Australia stumbles its way through the next two decades, and the City of Melton feels the negative effects of an economic downturn. Previous linear population growth is reduced to pockets of stalled development and local government revenue is down, limiting the ability of Council to control its own destiny with regard to spending. The status and influence of Council is diminished as state governments adopt an autocratic 'central command' approach to drive local government efficiencies.

In many respects, Australia is once again 'Living in the 1970s', stuttering along with an ill-fitting economy, high unemployment, disruptive union influence and decaying public infrastructure.

5. Building scenarios

Building scenarios is an exercise in creativity in which participants are challenged to develop a set of equally plausible futures that are strategically useful to management. The scenarios do *not* have to be individually distinct, but they *do* have to be diverse enough to generate different responses to the strategic challenge. The task for participants is to provide the detail within their scenarios that makes these differences explicit.

To achieve this goal, I've found the following seven-step process to be effective:

1. Develop a shared understanding of the scenario drivers.
2. Outline the scenario's top-line features.
3. Define the scenario's push and pull factors.
4. Describe the essence of the scenario.
5. Populate the scenario.
6. Backcast the scenario.
7. Write the scenario.

The first step is undertaken as a plenary group with the purpose of ensuring clarity around each of the scenario drivers and defining extreme, yet plausible, outcomes for each. The next three steps form a set whose purpose is to deepen each group's understanding and feel for their scenario *before* they begin the actual process of bringing it to life. This platform should ensure a smooth transition to fleshing out the scenario in step 5, providing the detail that enables managerial judgement in relation to the strategic challenge. Step 6 connects the future back to today via a backcasting process, which describes a plausible pathway of how the end-scenario came to be. The events and outcomes outlined in this process provide the framework for ongoing organisational scanning. Finally, the scenarios are written up as short stories of the future.

I will illustrate this process by using actual output from the MacGyver scenario team in the Melton City Council project in order to demonstrate the *anatomy* of scenario building in a workshop setting. Throughout these steps I offer my own comments and interpretation of the raw output to give an insight into the thinking and analysis that contributed to the eventual scenario plot.

STEP 1: DEVELOP A SHARED UNDERSTANDING OF THE SCENARIO DRIVERS

The critical drivers that form the scenario axes provide the framework in which the scenarios are developed. It is therefore essential to ensure from the outset a shared understanding of what is meant by each driver, lest you begin building scenarios with group members holding different interpretations in their minds. Failure to develop this understanding can eventually unravel the process through a combination of confusion and inconsistency.

Participants in the Melton City Council workshop began their scenario building by addressing the following questions as a plenary group:

- What do we mean by a *high level / low level* of local government autonomy?
- What do we mean by a *high-performing/low-performing* economy?

Since these axes effectively pull your scenarios apart, it is important to encourage thinking that lies at the plausible extremes for each dimension, thus optimising the broad differences between the scenarios and laying the groundwork for different managerial considerations and strategic responses. Thinking in terms of plausible extremes also ensures that your scenarios cover the broad 'envelope of uncertainty' for the strategic challenge.[9] This coverage is both logical and critical when you relate it to the use of scenario planning by emergency services. These organisations don't prepare for slight deviations from the norm for which they can easily adapt; they plan for extremes — scenarios that will seriously challenge or break their existing processes and capabilities. It's the same with scenarios in business: their purpose is to prepare the organisation for when it matters most.

In encouraging *stretch* in participants' thinking, I often ask attendees to bring to the workshop an image that represents an activity, policy or phrase from the past that was once considered acceptable but today appears ridiculous. Historical images of doctors promoting cigarettes always lighten the mood, and this is a relaxed way of commencing day two. There is a method in the madness, though: if we view many aspects of past behaviour as ridiculous, then we can assume that people in the future will view many aspects of our current behaviour as equally ridiculous. Therefore, looking forward, we must accept that many aspects of the future may appear ridiculous from the context of today. The learning for participants is that they should include plausible stretch and novelty in their scenarios.

The responses to this first step appear in tables 10.3 and 10.4 (overleaf).

Table 10.3: what do we mean by level of economic performance?

High-performing economy	Low-performing economy
High level of investment — private and public	Dormant development — low capital investment
Low unemployment	Higher unemployment, particularly among youth and minorities
Strong wages growth and high disposable income	Low wages growth
High population growth / immigration	Slower population growth

(continued)

Table 10.3: what do we mean by level of economic performance? *(cont'd)*

Increased diversity of services available	Mortgage stress and defaults
Strong housing growth	Small business failures affecting Main Street
High standard of living and expectations	Slowed planning rate — patchy, uncoordinated
Industry and employment diversity	Widening wealth distribution gap
Greater investment in innovation, technology, science and education	Increased demand for social services (family violence and mental health services)

Table 10.4: what do we mean by level of local government autonomy?

High level of local government autonomy	Low level of local government autonomy
No state government cap on council rates	Little influence on policy, service delivery, land use, planning, fiscal management
Increased volatility of Council decisions — potential broader range of services delivered	Local government becomes another government department
Less prescription by *Local Government Act* (being told what to do), more guidelines	Less responsive and engaged with local community
More entrepreneurial organisation	Financial constraints determined by state government
Greater influence over issues such as roads, schools, public transport	Services directed by federal and state governments
Increased local decision making / data collection	Less capacity to respond to external environment (e.g. climate change, economy)
Total control over rates / fees and charges / expenditure	New impositions placed on local government (e.g. shared services)
Service delivery models determined by Council	No councillors

STEP 2: OUTLINE THE SCENARIO'S TOP-LINE FEATURES

Breaking back into their smaller workshop teams, participants began the process of building their individual scenarios by defining the broad features of their future based on the *combination* of their scenario drivers. This combination is key: it is the frame of reference through which participants develop their scenarios.

This step is designed to ensure shared understanding among group members of the type of scenario about to be created, while outlining the broad aspects that will provide scaffolding for the eventual scenario plot.

MacGyver scenario output

The MacGyver scenario was developed within the framework of a low-performing economy and high level of local government autonomy. Responses from the scenario team appear below:

Top-line scenario features:

- innovation/community-led industries
- change in volunteerism
- local focus—we determine what we deliver
- higher accountability to local community than to state minister
- less government grants
- higher community expectations of Council delivery
- greater control over resource allocation—what we do and how we do it
- high unemployment rate
- increased demand for social and welfare services
- more agile organisation due to higher rate of change.

Comment — interpretation

From a scenario analysis perspective, early themes to emerge from this step include:

- the shift in Council accountability from state government to local community
- the community's expectation that local government representation (e.g. services) will be more specific to the wants of the community (*local focus*)
- the need to be agile in response to more dynamic community demands (*agile organisation*)
- the community's optimism and ingenuity in overcoming economic challenges (*innovation/community-led industries*)
- the willingness of the community to work together (*change in volunteerism*)
- the need to be a leaner and more entrepreneurial organisation in order to be more financially autonomous (*less government grants*).

STEP 3: DEFINE THE SCENARIO'S PUSH AND PULL FACTORS

In this step you address *why* this scenario would develop. Identifying the push and pull factors that could lead to your scenario outcomes grounds the scenario in the uncertainty of today's embryonic and emerging drivers. The connection back to today establishes plausibility at the base of the scenario, providing a credible platform from which to launch your scenario narrative (see figure 10.11). Once again, an effective environmental scan should provide the necessary stimulus for participants to determine their scenario push and pull factors.

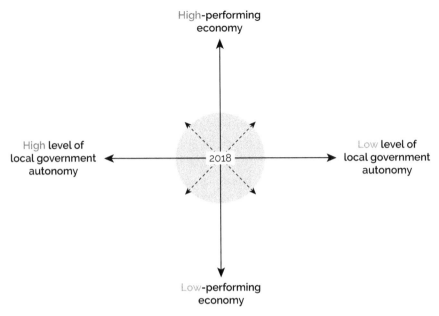

Figure 10.11: defining scenario push and pull factors

Defining scenario push and pull factors grounds the storylines in the uncertainty of today's embryonic and emerging drivers, establishing the platform for plausible scenario narratives.

MacGyver scenario output

Why would a low-performing economy / high level of local government autonomy scenario develop?

- Community resistance to being 'dictated to' by a big central government
- Government policy that provides for autonomy
- Downturn in world markets
- Failure to address key economic vulnerabilities
- Economic warfare
- Bursting of housing 'bubble'
- Interest rate rises, inflation
- Impact of ageing, non-working population

- State government economy underpinned by land tax, stamp duty and GST distribution—if they change, it could affect Victoria's economy.

Comment—interpretation

The trend of communities wanting greater emphasis on local issues from their elected representatives became a strong scenario theme and provided the pull factor for greater local government autonomy (*community resistance to big-government 'dictating'*). This storyline was inspired by the Brexit campaign and the pushback by UK residents against Brussels and the European Union.

Economic warfare was interpreted as a trade war caused by economic protectionism that damages Australian exports and ultimately causes a slowdown in economic performance. These economic factors provided the push factors for increased local government autonomy.

Subsequent pressure on state government revenues emerged as a driver of cost-shifting, as local governments took on more and more responsibility (*state government economy underpinned by land tax, stamp duty etc.*).

STEP 4: DESCRIBE THE ESSENCE OF THE SCENARIO

With the scenario essence, you're asking participants to give a sense of their scenario's *look and feel*. Is it a dystopian scenario? A technological scenario? A scenario of widening social and economic disparities? In my experience, this exercise has proven invaluable in bringing the less tangible elements of the scenario to the surface. Sure, there are lots of physical and measurable changes in your scenario, but *what are people feeling?* And how might these feelings then lead to subsequent developments within your scenario? It's an understanding of the intangible look and feel of a scenario that often leads to richer storylines and the surfacing of deeper insights.

Following this step, participants should have an intrinsic feel for the logic of their scenario, prepared to flesh out their storylines with a clear understanding of why the scenario evolved, what it looks like, how different stakeholders are feeling and how they might behave in such circumstances.

MacGyver scenario output

What does this scenario look and feel like?

- Economically bleak (boarded-up shopfronts etc.)
- Grassroots innovation
- Lots of opportunities to 'make a difference'
- More scrutiny and visibility of government actions
- Likely run-down in assets
- Disengagement from state government
- Stagnating development areas
- Council becomes more entrepreneurial
- Council looks for potential for agility
- Community wants more Council leadership
- Common interests drive communal behaviour and open-mindedness
- World of opportunity for community and Council
- Higher appetite for risk in trying new things / innovation.

Comment — interpretation

This starts to feel like a scenario where the community accepts their challenges with optimism and a 'can do' attitude (*lots of opportunities to 'make a difference'; world of opportunity; grassroots innovation*).

The output here also gives a sense of resourcefulness (*likely run-down in assets; Council looks for potential for agility*), entrepreneurialism, ingenuity (*higher appetite for risk in trying new things*) and collaboration (*common interests drive communal behaviour*).

The opportunity in this scenario is for Council to play a leadership role within the community in the key areas of optimism, resourcefulness, entrepreneurialism, ingenuity and collaboration (*community wants more Council leadership*).

STEP 5: POPULATE THE SCENARIO

Fleshing out your scenario starts by defining the broad domains you want to describe that are relevant to the strategic challenge. These domains can include the economy, technology, government, consumers and, of course, relevant stakeholders.

In building the Melton City Council scenarios, the focus was on the following scenario components and stakeholders:

- social
- technology
- economy
- environment
- politics
- Melton community
- local government
- state government.

It's then useful to work through a series of questions (not too many) to guide and prompt participants in bringing each of these domains to life. Your objective here is to provide just enough structure to facilitate a relevant strategic conversation around each of the components. I'm not going to list all of the questions from this workshop. However, I will mention that in designing your questions, it's important to focus on the areas you want participants to address explicitly—what details are needed to enable managerial judgement? This includes all *critical planning issues* and relevant *important scenario drivers* from the impact/uncertainty matrix—remember, no important influencing factor gets left behind.

The following are examples of questions relating to the social domain:

- What are the priorities or concerns of people in your scenario?
- Which significant lifestyle behaviours are different in your scenario vs today?
- What new infrastructure exists to support 2036 lifestyles?
- What are the challenges for people in this scenario? How are these challenges overcome?

Again, these questions are only a guide to get people started and to provide some structure to the scenario building process. In fact, what you find with the intuitive logics approach is that participants soon realise the interconnectedness of their scenario — that changes in one domain, say the economy, have multiple impacts across other domains. So rather than following the scenario questions in a linear fashion, a natural flow begins to develop whereby participants build their scenarios in a non-linear, organic way, focusing simultaneously on cause-and-effect relationships across all domains (*If this happens, then I can see how this and this could also happen*). Soon enough, a logical and coherent scenario should begin to emerge.

STEP 6: BACKCAST THE SCENARIO

Backcasting is a process that connects your scenarios back to the present, outlining a plausible pathway of events and outcomes that could contribute to the development of each end-state — a history of the future, if you like. Once again, this is an exercise in plausible creativity. The purpose is to outline a logical and plausible sequence of events and outcomes that demonstrate, 'Look, this could happen'.

In some respects backcasting is the most challenging aspect of the scenarios process. Convincing management that extreme scenarios could affect their operations is not so difficult; much more challenging is describing a plausible pathway that shows *how* these scenarios could develop. This plausibility is the benchmark if scenarios are to be accepted as legitimate. It is central to driving action.

Backcasting imperatives

There are a couple of imperatives for effective backcasting:

1. The pathway should link the significant themes in your end-scenario back to the push and pull factors identified in step 3.
2. The pathway should be plausible and logical. Does it make sense from a cause-and-effect perspective? Is the chronological order of events logical?

Abiding by these stipulations, participants should consider any number of factors across the iSTEEP categories that could have contributed to their scenario development. As long as it makes sense, nothing is out of bounds.

Consider recent developments in the Australian dairy industry and how they affected the critical uncertainty of milk prices for farmers.[10] In April 2016 Murray Goulburn, Australia's largest milk processor, suddenly announced that it was retrospectively dropping the milk price it would pay dairy farmers by more than 10 per cent. The move shocked suppliers, who were given no warning that such a change was about to take place. Farmers who had made substantial investments based on the old price now found themselves owing back-pay to Murray Goulburn, as well as trying to service their loans on the lower milk price. What is interesting from a scenario planning perspective is how this outcome came about.

Most milk produced in the southern parts of Australia is processed into cheese and milk powders for export. Hence, the global dairy market is the key driver of the price paid to farmers. Each financial year Murray Goulburn would set milk prices and if there was a positive fluctuation in price during the year, the processor would lift prices and retrospectively back pay farmers the difference. So far, so good.

In February/March 2014, the Crimean peninsula was annexed from Ukraine by Russia, sparking outcry from the West and the subsequent imposition of trade and travel bans. In July 2014, tensions rose further after Malaysia Airlines flight MH17 was shot down over eastern Ukraine and suspicion fell on pro-Russia rebels. As a result, the United

States, the European Union, Australia and other countries imposed even tougher economic sanctions on Russia.

Russia responded with its own ban on Western imports, including dairy products. European dairy products previously destined for Russia were now being exported to markets where Australia was a major supplier.

Compounding matters, in March 2015 the European Union withdrew its dairy production quota, which had been used to cap rising milk production since the early 1980s. Milk production subsequently increased and prices fell. Then, to complete the perfect storm, in early 2016 it was revealed that China had excess supplies of milk powder, which placed even greater pressure on Australian exports.

Murray Goulburn eventually succumbed to the combined impact of these global forces and in April 2016 announced a retrospective cut in farmer milk prices.

Now, how's that for a complex and intriguing scenario?

The point is, there are countless ways that a scenario can develop. It doesn't really matter how your scenario outcomes evolve, as long as the pathway is plausible and logical—*does it make sense from a cause-and-effect perspective?*

The results of the environmental scan are particularly useful during this exercise, because this is where your understanding of how the system works today—what it relies on, what it is susceptible to and where the potential fault lines are—can be critical to generating a plausible narrative.

Backcasting delivers several benefits

- **Plausibility.** Backcasting provides the essential test of logic and plausibility for each scenario: Given what has to occur to enable our scenarios to eventuate, how feasible are these events and outcomes within the scenario horizon?

For example, public opinion takes time to change and is influenced by unfolding events; political decisions take time to legislate; and infrastructure takes time and resources to build. If this chain of events is not plausible within your scenario horizon, then you might need to explore a new series of events leading to the same outcome, or your end-scenario might need to be reviewed.

- **Sensitivity.** Backcasting delivers ongoing environmental sensitivity by providing a framework for future scanning. In this respect, backcasting provides a context for scanning by outlining the future signposts that have significance for the strategic challenge — you now know what to look for. The use and value of these signposts is discussed in detail in chapter 13.

- **Understanding.** Backcasting deepens your understanding of the scenario. As you work through the process, you become immersed in the unfolding scenario, taking on the roles of various actors, their motivations and likely actions. This deeper understanding leads to greater clarity about what could happen in the future and why.

Backcasting process

1. **Identify the significant themes or features of your end-scenario.** These are the themes or developments with significance for the strategic challenge — the differences that make a difference. Each group should agree on up to four significant features and label these clearly.

2. **Outline bridging events.** What's required to *bridge* the difference between your scenario features and today?

For each of the significant themes or features, list the factors or events that could enable these to develop. What could or must occur? Why would these events occur? Capture these factors on individual Post-it notes. Use the iSTEEP categories as a guide to ensure a spread of relevant factors:

- **Industry.** Which industry developments could have led to these features?
- **Social.** What social pressures could assist the development of your scenario themes?
- **Technological.** What technology is required? How is it being used?
- **Economic.** What infrastructure is necessary? When would this infrastructure be built?
- **Environmental.** What environmental events could have led to these outcomes?
- **Political.** What regulations or government policies need to be implemented?

Once this list appears complete, place the events in the chronological order in which they might occur by moving the Post-it notes around according to the logic of cause and effect. As you go through this process, new events are likely to continue to emerge. Finally, review the flow of your storyline. Does it seem plausible? (see figure 10.12)

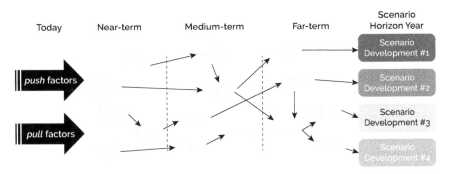

Figure 10.12: scenario backcast

The scenario backcast links the significant themes in your end-scenario back to today's push and pull factors via a plausible and logical pathway.

These backcasting events and their outcomes are now the key to organisational sensitivity, providing the relevant signals for ongoing environmental scanning. The art and act of undertaking this scanning is described further in chapter 13.

STEP 7: WRITE THE SCENARIO

Writing scenarios is an immersive and reflective process that facilitates the generation of fresh insights. It's a process that enables the scenario writer to step inside different worlds and to develop an in-depth feel for their drivers, characteristics and distinctions. Such immersion can be the most rewarding part of the process, drawing on the dual skills of analysis and creativity to uncover and express new insights in a manner that aids managerial judgement.

In this respect, scenario writing and scenario analysis are seriously intertwined. As you can see from the sample output I've provided throughout this chapter, the time constraints of a workshop mean scenario insights don't necessarily drop into your lap in the form of a cohesive storyline. Instead, depending on your workshop format, they tend to be captured in abbreviated or bullet point form, challenging the writer to discover the sometimes hidden themes that weave through the story.

Active listening during the workshop is the requisite behaviour to rise to this challenge: What were the group conversations? What were the contexts in which these conversations took place? What were people's emotions when they spoke on certain issues? The scenario writer has to be in a position to use this recall to complement the actual workshop output. The skill is then to use your creativity to re-express this output in a manner consistent with your scenario storyline while staying true to the essence of the group's intent.

As your scenario takes shape, you soon find yourself immersed in a future world. And with this immersion, a clear simplicity emerges, so you begin to rely less on the actual workshop output and instead use your natural feel for the scenario to broaden and develop its storylines.

Betty Sue Flowers, the former scenario writer at Shell, articulating this effect in her article 'The art and strategy of scenario writing', writes:

> In the course of distilling one of the 1992 scenarios, which described the resistance to globalization, I was left with the image of 'barricades'—the title of the scenario itself. 'Barricades'—the title and the image of resistance—was like a seed from which you could grow the entire story.[11]

As a consequence of this immersion and 'distilling', further insights on scenario implications and opportunities continue to surface (see figure 10.13).

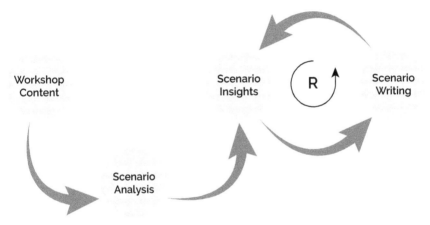

Figure 10.13: scenario writing and analysis

Scenario writing and analysis are intertwined, with your initial scenario insights providing the basis for your storyline, while the immersive activity of writing leads to newer insights.

Writing effective scenarios

Similar to the environmental scan, but with one significant difference, the only useful scenario is one that is read, considered, shared *and acted upon*. Here are some leads on writing an effective scenario.

- **Enable judgement.** Your scenarios should contain enough detail to enable managerial judgements in relation to the strategic challenge. Your goal here, writes futurist Jamais Cascio, 'is to make sure that what you think they [decision makers] need to know is what comes across in the scenario'.[12] In doing so, your scenarios should provide an outline of what could happen without being too detailed or specific — remember, you're not trying to predict the future.

- **If one door shuts, another must open.** The scenario should highlight both the challenges and the opportunities for the organisation. For example, in a scenario in which the organisation's current business model is challenged, it's not enough simply to highlight that the business will be in trouble if it continues to do what it does; this will be obvious and not helpful. Your scenario should also provide enough detail to make alternative choices and applications of the organisation's capabilities apparent: *What other opportunities are relevant to our business?*

- **Describe the journey.** Don't simply focus on the end-scenario; describe the plausible journey showing *how* this scenario came to be and highlighting the events and outcomes that led from today to the future. Similar outcomes may involve very different journeys, inviting different decisions from the organisation along the way.

- **'Keep it short.'** This advice was delivered to Betty Sue Flowers by the head of Group Planning on her first day as scenario editor at Shell, and I think it's the key to ensuring a scenario is both useful and usable.[13] Just as in an environmental scan, denseness is the greatest impediment to readability and usefulness. The scenarios must be digestible for those who were involved in their development and those who weren't. Of course, with the key decision makers involved in the actual process of developing the scenarios, there's no need for the narratives to be too long. The scenarios are merely a cohesive articulation of *their* thinking. And don't make the mistake of overcompensating with content for those who weren't involved, as this will have the reverse effect — your scenarios just won't be read.

- **Make the name 'sticky'.** In naming your scenarios try to capture the essence of your story in a word, a phrase or a metaphor. These names should be easy to remember and enable people to recall the essence of the scenario through word association. There's no need to come up with a particularly clever scenario name; often a simple word that captures the key scenario themes is best for ongoing internal communication.

- **Take your time.** Finally, allow enough time to step inside each scenario and permit ideas and concepts to percolate and develop. I try to allow a minimum six weeks between the scenarios workshop and the follow-up workshop on strategic positioning to give myself enough time to fully understand and express the different insights within each scenario. As mentioned earlier, the future clarity and new insights that emerge from scenario immersion can be among the most satisfying aspects of the project.

MacGyver scenario example

This scenario is defined by community resourcefulness, self-sufficiency and ingenuity. It's about making the most of what you have. The name refers to the 1980s television series *MacGyver*, whose lead character epitomised resourcefulness, agility, inventiveness and unconventional problem-solving.

Narrative

The MacGyver scenario taps into the growing backlash against globalisation and the increasing desire for greater local or community agency that has been expressed by voters across the globe in recent years. We saw this trend play out in the US presidential elections of 2016 when millions of 'forgotten' voters who felt disempowered by globalisation and disenfranchised by the political system supported Donald Trump all the way to the White House. And in the June 2016 UK Brexit referendum we again saw a pushback from communities who were tired of being 'dictated to' by a big central government in Brussels.

After a sustained period of outward-looking global economic policies, and with trust in the political process at an all-time low, voters are taking a sledgehammer to remind politicians of who they actually work for.

As a consequence of this new focus on localisation, the increasing economic protectionism first signalled by Donald Trump during his presidential campaign and then enacted via US trade tariffs on China in early 2018 is soon escalated by retaliatory responses from China. A sustained trade war ensues, as other countries go down the protectionism path, stifling global economic growth.

Australia finds itself exposed to the new protectionist dynamic and the subsequent downturn in export demand affects the local economy. This has a flow-on effect in the domestic building and construction industries. Unemployment begins to rise and the 'housing bubble' bursts, causing housing development in the suburbs to stall.

Feeling squeezed by decreased revenues, state governments increasingly look to shift costs, giving more and more responsibility to local governments. These economic circumstances represent the push factors for greater local government autonomy.

This increased responsibility is welcomed by local communities, as it satisfies their growing desire for greater local representation and agency. Their expectation is that increased local government autonomy will lead to services and infrastructure that better meet the specific needs of their region ('We determine what we deliver and how we deliver it'). In this scenario, community expectations of Council delivery remain high despite the constrained economic circumstances. This community-driven trend towards greater communal independence and representation provides the pull factor for greater local government autonomy.

Accordingly, Council gains more control over resource allocation and more levers to respond to whatever conditions arise, while having greater accountability for local economic performance.

The creative and collaborative habits formed during this scenario lay the groundwork for future long-term economic recovery as Australia emerges from a bloated, disposable culture to become an efficient and innovative twenty-first-century economy.

Community

This is a scenario in which the community has to work together and be innovative to solve issues brought on by lack of funding and rising costs. Such constrained conditions help bind the community together, creating a stronger sense of community spirit.

Furthermore, a positive and innovative outlook permeates the community. People do not see lower economic growth as a constraint, but rather as a challenge to be overcome. In this respect, the world is full of opportunities and there is a stronger appetite to try new things and innovate to make a positive difference ('Necessity is the mother of invention').

Habits are generally more frugal in 2036. People tend to grow at least a portion of their own vegetables, and community gardens are scattered throughout the city. There is increased demand for public resources including transport, education and health services. Car sharing is much more widely adopted compared with 2018.

Club memberships of all kinds grow as participation in recreational and sporting activities increases. This is a scenario in which people want to belong to communities of common interest.

There is a strong belief in making a positive contribution to the community and increased volunteerism, particularly among those under 40.

There is higher demand for shared public spaces and community facilities and a greater willingness among organisations to share recreational facilities and to utilise informal public spaces for formal participation purposes.

Economy

The economic landscape is challenging, with high unemployment, low capital investment, low interest rates, low wages growth and many small business closures.

The economy is dominated by more frugal attitudes towards consumption and the aspiration of many to pay down debt. This behaviour places further downward pressure on inflation and interest rates and reduces per capita GST revenue for the states.

There is a booming sharing economy, which represents a further example of an innovative response to challenging circumstances. People are comfortable with repurposing assets and goods, and the disposable culture is a thing of the past. This attitude extends from personal possessions to community assets, where the emphasis is on using existing infrastructure assets to the maximum. 'Sweat the assets!' is the mantra for the times.

The building and construction industries have declined since 2018 and there is less mobility and fewer transactions in the housing sector, affecting stamp duty receipts for state governments. Unemployment is higher, particularly among youth and minorities. Underemployment flatters the unemployment number, as many overqualified people are forced to take on lesser roles. Many others are forced to work multiple jobs or to freelance their skills to make ends meet. Mortgage stress is an issue throughout the community and loan defaults are not uncommon.

Discretionary spend (retail, lifestyle services) and luxury industries have declined, as people spend more of their time 'doing', particularly undertaking activities that are free and local, such as socialising with friends.

Organisations place a greater emphasis on reducing costs and inefficiencies, and actively seek out opportunities to collaborate with partners with complementary capabilities.

There is less transience in the workplace, with people prioritising job security. Accordingly, more and more employees are choosing to work beyond the age of 70. Workers seek refuge in unions, which become more powerful political operatives. Manufacturing and construction become more prone to union unrest and strikes, further destabilising Australia's economic competitiveness.

Politics and governance

With less reliance on external grants, the focus of local government is on efficient and sustainable communal solutions. This requires Council to be more entrepreneurial, resourceful and creative. Services are rationalised, shared service models operate throughout the state, and councils collaborate with public and private partners to take out costs and inefficiencies in business operations.

With greater accountability for local economic development and Council economic autonomy, we see the 'corporatisation' of local government practices and a greater emphasis on entrepreneurial management styles to seek out alternate sources of income. A changing perspective of Council debt may place a greater emphasis on risk management as entrepreneurial managers accustomed to working with higher debt levels look to secure capacity through debt.

The shift to more autonomous local government, which effectively moves the decision-making process closer to the people, successfully closes the trust deficit between the public and politicians that had become a chasm in 2018.

Finally, having achieved more autonomous local representation, the community now has higher expectations of Council delivery *(Be careful what you wish for)*.

Melton

With sporadic and patchy population growth, public assets need to be 'agile' so as to deliver optimal community value and usage. This means there is greater multipurpose usage throughout the city and throughout the day, and residents and associations have successfully adapted to this sharing culture.

There is greater demand for social services, including family violence and mental health services, but the deeper sense of community spirit guarantees a strong emphasis on community welfare provision. We see an example of this spirit in the upsurge in local volunteers since 2018.

With a more proactive approach to sustainability, individuals and neighbourhoods take personal responsibility for home front environmental issues and have high expectations of government to do the same.

Evaluating the scenarios

So, after all that effort, how do you judge whether a scenario exercise has actually been successful or not? Well, it's not about how well the scenarios are written; how structured, logical or comprehensive their content; how memorable their names; or how novel they appear to the outsider ('I could have done better than that'). The scenarios themselves are merely the means to an end. And the *end* against which scenarios should be judged is this: *Did they make a positive impact?* For this reason, the success or otherwise of a scenario process can be judged only by the intended users of the product.

In saying that, I believe there are three criteria by which scenario exercises can be assessed:

1. **Insight:** Were new perceptions generated?
2. **Impact:** Were these insights acted upon?
3. **Judgement:** Were better decisions made?

Unless these criteria are met, the exercise is likely to prove a disappointment. The goodwill and enthusiasm generated throughout the process ('This is different') will quickly dissipate, and good luck trying to gather support for any future efforts ('Fool me once...'). Unfortunately, this is where many scenario processes end up: overpromising and underdelivering, leaving management and participants unsatisfied. My early efforts certainly did.

Of course, the final criterion, *better decisions*, can only be assessed over time, within the context of specific objectives being achieved. And before this assessment can take place, the scenarios must first drive *action*. This means addressing the *so what?* and *now what?* challenges.

CHAPTER 11

'So what?' — Positioning for the future

The limitations of contextual intelligence are exposed when novel environments emerge

'Why don't we offer them a scenario planning project?' I suggested to the NSW Sales Manager at Foster's in early 2006. 'Them' being one of our major customers, a large hospitality and entertainment business with multiple venues throughout New South Wales. I had been in my role as National Foresight Manager for about six months, and it had often occurred to me that our growing scenarios capability was something we might be able to take to customers as a value-add offering that couldn't be replicated by our competitors. Upcoming contract negotiations for the next term of beer pourage rights provided the perfect opportunity to test my theory. Foster's beer brands had a minority presence in these venues, and a favourable change in trading terms would be a great win for our NSW sales team and a huge boost to the profile of foresight within Foster's.

The client's management were excited, so we went all out. A three-day workshop was scheduled, venues were hired, catering was ordered, and flights and accommodation booked. We even hired a university undergraduate to record the entire three days with a view to editing a short film of our efforts — a snapshot of our unprecedented collaboration. No expense was spared.

Over three days, teams comprising executives from both organisations jointly created scenarios and considered responses for the decade ahead. Expectations were high as the output was collated. I took it away, promising to return in five weeks with the final report.

The great unveil was a major letdown. It started badly when the volume for the video didn't work and went downhill from there. The report was nothing more than a virtual rehash of the notes taken during the workshop, with little analysis and no new insights or recommendations. It was merely a collection of underdeveloped ideas written down under the time constraints of a workshop. No effort had been made to turn these ideas into a coherent and compelling strategic argument. No subsequent strategic action could possibly be tied back to what was presented. I had failed the 'so what?' test.

Despite their diplomacy, the client's disappointment was unmistakable. Not surprisingly, when the new pourage rights agreement was signed, the CEO thanked the Foster's team for their efforts, but there was to be no improvement in the presence of our beer brands. As for the 18 hours of uncut workshop footage, it's probably still collecting dust in a back office somewhere at Foster's — a sad metaphor for the exercise.

It's called scenario *planning*

This ill-fated project is a classic example of the scenarios cliché: promises are made, excitement is generated … and disappointment is delivered. Such ineffectiveness has prevented the practice from being adopted more widely. And it's largely a self-inflicted wound.

Looking back, it's obvious that I was content to operate in the *safe* 'what's next?' phase of scenario planning. I was more focused on the scenarios than on the planning, which is ultimately what's relevant to the client. Unsurprisingly, this is a common error for people who enter the futures field; after all, they're drawn to scenarios through an interest in understanding how the future could be different. But to be organisationally relevant, a scenario planner must move beyond any single-minded focus on 'what's next?' as quickly as possible. No matter how accurate your scenarios might ultimately turn out to be, any exercise fails if it merely leads your client to shrug 'so what?' and take no action. Successful scenario planners take responsibility for driving action-oriented outcomes. Regrettably it took me years to realise this.

With my focus firmly on the future, my responsibilities, as I saw them, extended only so far as helping clients to understand what could happen externally. As for making strategic sense from these scenarios, well, that was someone else's responsibility. It's as if my attitude was: 'Here you go…I've done my job. I've told you what could happen. Surely you senior managers are clever enough to make sense of it; after all, you're the experts.'

Except sometimes they're not.

Anyone for chess?

In the 1940s, Dutch psychologist A. D. de Groot studied the cognitive abilities of chess players of varying levels of skill.[1] His goal was to identify the reasons that explained the playing differences between the masters and the amateurs. An answer lay in the masters' ability to memorise the layout of pieces on a chess board. Given only seconds to look, master players could accurately reconstruct the layout they had just seen. The recall of amateur players was significantly lower.

Harvard University professor David Perkins explains one reason for this disparity[2]:

With experience in a domain, people learn to encode the world in larger chunks that hang together. A chess master, for instance, will not just perceive piece by piece, but will see larger configurations of pieces—a rook on an open file, a fork accomplished by a knight. Able to encode the arrangement of the pieces in the vocabulary of these larger chunks, the master can take in an entire board in the form of a few chunks … providing the arrangement is natural to chess.

But what happens when the landscape changes? When new patterns emerge that no longer match the contextual intelligence of the expert?

De Groot asked himself the same question and his findings have major implications for scenario planners and strategy development. Before performing the test again, de Groot placed the pieces in unconventional positions on the chess board. This time the masters produced amateur results.

It appears the masters had a contextual expertise. As long as the game was played according to traditional paradigms, where the patterns were recognisable, they could apply their contextual knowledge. The lessons here can be applied to strategic thinking. We often say an experienced senior manager has vast industry intelligence, when what they really have is vast *contextual* intelligence. Their expertise relates to 'what is' but not necessarily to 'what could be'. As long as the context in which they are asked to make judgements is familiar, they can apply their contextual intelligence intuitively (unconscious competence).

The limitations of this intelligence can be exposed when scenarios present different, future contexts, reducing managerial capability from unconscious competence back to conscious incompetence (see figure 11.1). This is why it's not enough to simply present scenarios without addressing the 'so what?' challenge. To be effective you must also help your client to make the link between the key messages contained within the scenarios and the strategic implications and opportunities for their operations. Critical to making this link is understanding the organisation's strategic identity.

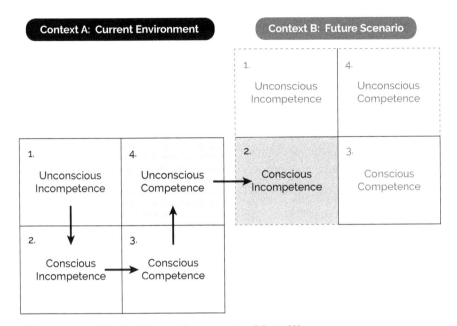

Figure 11.1: limitations of contextual intelligence

The four stages of competence learning model can be used to show how managerial competence is reduced when confronted with novel scenario environments.

Strategic identity

Detecting and attaching relevance to scenarios relies on drawing an affiliation with the organisation's sense of identity—*how it sees itself*. Naturally, the narrower or more rigid this internal sense of self, the harder it is to make strategic connections. On the other hand, the broader and more flexible the organisation's sense of identity, the easier it will be to perceive future opportunities and to reconceive its future self.

Organisational identity consists of several tiers, with the deeper layers underpinning the visible customer-facing activities performed by the enterprise (see figure 11.2, overleaf):

1. *What you do and how you do it* are the superficial activities of the organisation, the visible functions, products and services

that tend to define you in the eyes of outsiders ('Libraries are about books'; 'General Motors make cars'). These activities are not fixed; they simply represent a transient manifestation of the company's capabilities, vision and mission.

2. *Capabilities* refer to the combination of resources and competencies that enable an organisation's business operations. These capabilities can include intellectual property and skills, internal culture and processes, raw materials, infrastructure and assets, regulatory protection or external partnerships.

3. *Vision* refers to the scope of the organisation's ambition—what it wants to be or to achieve. It provides direction for future strategic priorities, objectives and actions.

4. The organisation's *mission* represents its purpose, its reason for being. It's at this level that the organisation's sense of identity is formed, as managers determine 'What business are we in?'

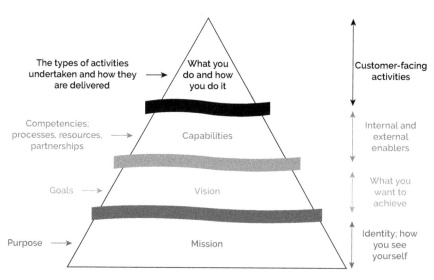

Figure 11.2: organisational identity pyramid

The organisation's sense of identity frames the direction of its purpose and the boundaries of its vision—'who we are and what we want to be'.

The organisation's sense of identity is the prism through which managers see the world. It acts as a sort of filter, determining the relevance you attach to changes in the external environment, and the range of activities you consider in response ('for us'/'not for us').[3]

Organisations get themselves into trouble when they have a narrow or rigid sense of identity that limits their ability to detect and respond to changes in the external environment. Typically, this occurs when managers view the organisation through its business activities at the tip of the identity pyramid, losing sight of their original or underlying purpose ('We are what we do'). These businesses tend to be swamped by change; lacking the sensitivity to detect impending shifts, and the leverage to reconceive what they could do, they keep doing the same thing despite declining relevance.

This is why addressing the internal 'so what?' question is just as important as addressing the external 'what's next?' challenge. There's no point developing scenarios that are great guides to the future only to have a bewildered management turn to you and say, 'That's all well and good, but how is it relevant to *us*? We sell computers!'

For organisations with a narrow sense of identity, scenarios tend to be viewed as either good or bad: good, if the existing business operations continue to appear legitimate in the future ('business as usual'); bad, if the scenarios paint a bleak picture for the future of current operations ('This isn't good for us'). This positive or negative interpretation is a common response to a scenario presentation, viewed as it is in the context of what the organisation does today. Such a superficial assessment paints the organisation into a corner, providing little leverage for internal change or innovation. However, as Kees van der Heijden points out, scenarios are neither good nor bad; they are 'only more of the same or different'.[4] The key to this change in perception lies in the organisation having a broad and flexible sense of its own identity, which allows it to detect and take advantage of these differences.

Such a perspective transforms organisational thinking beyond the traditional, bounded industry outlook, to thinking in terms of an unbounded and fluid transactional environment—'Where else are our capabilities scarce or in demand?' Adopting such a view opens up strategic options, as you invariably discover that the firm's capabilities are underutilised and that it has in fact been doing itself a disservice by limiting its focus to what it has always done. From an interpretation perspective, then, scenario differences actually present management with strategic opportunities and choices—'How best can we deploy our capabilities in the future?'

'WHAT BUSINESS ARE WE IN?'

Organisational purpose expressed as a mission statement remains misunderstood. Too often it is long-winded, too specific (detailing what the organisation intends to do) or aspirational (describing what it wants to be). Often it can stretch for a paragraph, the result of trying to appease all contributors in a formal planning environment. I've seen how these meetings can degenerate, despite the best intentions, into painstaking exercises as leaders agonise over words and grammar ('Shouldn't a comma go there?'), intellectually jostling to have their input immortalised in the final output.

Ultimately these mission statements prove ineffective. Rather than clarifying the organisation's sense of strategic identity, they leave people in a state of confusion, with no one completely satisfied with its expression, meaning or purpose. The mission is framed, displayed in the building's reception area and forgotten, serving little strategic purpose.

An effective organisational mission is:

- **broad**—as general as is practical, allowing flexibility to adapt operations as the environment changes, and opening up opportunities in compatible domains; as soon as you introduce specifics, you narrow your focus, and limit future options, thus threatening the organisation's durability

- **enduring**—a stable anchor that maintains relevance as the external environment changes

- **bridging**—enabling continuity between the organisation's past, present and future (true to your heritage ⟷ relevant to the future)
- **directional**—providing organisational clarity with regard to strategic intent and boundaries of interest ('We will invest our energies and resources in this direction')
- **succinct**—as brief as practical; your mission is about what you do, not how you do it
- **memorable**—easy to recall and articulate, and easy for others to comprehend.

BROADENING YOUR SENSE OF IDENTITY

Scenario interpretation is done from the level of strategic identity, so a *broad sense of identity* serves several strategic purposes (see figure 11.3):

- It optimises your capacity to attach *relevance* to your scenarios.
- It enhances your ability to extract strategic *significance* or *meaning* from your scenarios.
- It provides the essential leverage for strategic *flexibility* in response to your scenarios.

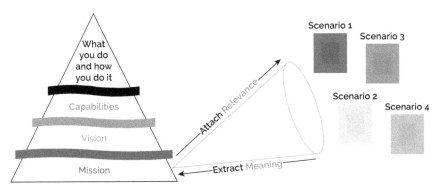

Figure 11.3: strategic identity and scenario interpretation

A broad sense of identity provides managers with the widest possible platform to attach relevance and draw strategic implications from scenarios.

Broadening your sense of identity allows the organisation to reframe the domains in which it sees itself competing (opportunities). Developing such a fresh perspective is the most effective way to trigger the internal paradigm shift necessary for strategic transformation. Without such a shift, new thinking and new action will rarely emerge.

In 2017 I was fortunate enough to be involved with a national roadshow of breakfast seminars for Toyota. Over the course of those two weeks I was introduced to their strategic purpose—'sustainable mobility solutions'—and, just as importantly, to the initiatives they had undertaken in support of this purpose.

Now, if you visit the website of any large motor vehicle company you're sure to come across the word 'mobility'. Almost simultaneously, and perhaps spurred on by the global financial crisis of 2008, it seemed that every car company had broadened their sense of strategic identity to 'providing mobility solutions'. What impressed me most about Toyota was how they were not just talking the talk but were truly walking the walk. The upframing[5] to sustainable mobility solutions was driving innovations in the domains of in-home mobility and human support robotics. With the Western world's population entering an unprecedented period of ageing, and personal mobility needs set to become a significant growth market over coming decades, this seemed a foresightful strategic move.

Focusing on 'mobility' enabled Toyota to seamlessly transcend its historical operations and improve its future relevance by competing for a larger piece of the mobility pie. And all of this while remaining true to its heritage—Toyota has always been in the business of providing mobility solutions.

Broadening your sense of identity is essentially about deepening your understanding of the question 'What business are we in?', the objective being to provide the broadest practical platform from which the organisation can face the future—you upframe first and assess any capability gaps second. One of the keys to reaching this platform is acknowledging the ultimate benefits of the organisation's operations:

- What are the ultimate benefits we deliver or contribute to?
- For what purpose do we do what we do?

Over the past 20 years the traditional printing industry has been challenged by technological developments, globalisation, industry consolidation, digitisation and the growth in 'superstore' competitors who can provide services at a cheaper rate. As a consequence, the number of operators in the industry has contracted considerably.

For those operators who saw themselves through the limiting lens of manufacturing and supplying printing materials, there was little room to move as this tsunami of change struck. However, those who acknowledged that their business functioned as a vehicle for their customers' broader marketing and communications purposes were able to reconceive their operations to remain relevant.

One such company that continues to thrive despite the industry turmoil is Lithocraft, a medium-sized operator based in Melbourne's western suburbs. Reading the changing business landscape correctly, management quickly realised that their previous mission to be 'a quality print provider and manufacturer' did not provide enough leverage to broaden their activities in a contracting market. Recognising that they were actually in the business of 'marketing communications and services' enabled management to move the organisation into adjacent opportunity domains including consulting, design, branding, campaign management, workflow and data management, print production (local and offshore) and finishing, retail displays, and warehousing and distribution.

Of course, the benefits you provide can be either tangible (as in the mobility example) or intangible.

Agricultural and horticultural (A&H) societies are institutions that tend to exist on the periphery of their communities. Most people have heard of them, but few know exactly what they do beyond organising an annual show at the local showgrounds. Born in an era when towns were built to service agricultural communities, and now affected by rapid urbanisation with urban sprawl infringing on traditional agricultural areas, A&H societies can suffer from a crisis of identity that extends to the boardrooms of the societies themselves—'Just who are we and where do we fit in?'

It was in this context that I was asked in 2018 to help an A&H society design its next five-year strategy. At the core of the challenge was establishing a sense of identity that was true to the society's purpose, gave it relevance beyond hosting the annual community show and provided direction for a coherent future strategy.

In developing this strategic mission, it was helpful to revisit the original purpose of these institutions, which was primarily to organise events that brought people together 'to enrich life in agricultural areas'.[6] This was the insight that was needed. The society's new mission was 'to enrich our community'. It was a purpose that was not only true to their heritage. It was easy to articulate, it was easy to comprehend, and it provided clear boundaries around what was *for us* or *not for us*. Most importantly, it opened up a vast array of potential domains in which they could play, thereby improving relevance to their local community. Arranging community events to facilitate social belonging and engagement, coordinating local volunteering efforts, working with education facilities to promote environmental awareness, or collaborating with the local business chamber to drive economic activity—basically any activities seen as beneficial to the community—could now be considered as being 'in play' under the umbrella of *enriching our community*.

CASE STUDY

'What is a public library in 2030?'[7]

In 2012 I was handed a 12-month project that many of my friends regarded as the easiest job in the world: working with the State Library of Victoria to design a long-term strategic framework for the state's library network. The purpose of this project was to address the strategic challenge: 'What is a public library in 2030?' 'That's easy,' they'd mocked, 'Libraries won't exist in the future because books won't exist.'

From the dismissive responses of my friends it was clear that despite all the changes public libraries had incorporated in recent years, the overwhelming external perception remained anchored in the past: libraries were passive warehouses for books ruled over by stern matronly types who were forever demanding people to *'Shoosh!'*

Regardless, it was hard to argue with their point. The world was changing rapidly, books and newspapers were increasingly digitised, and access to information was hardly a social scarcity. Across Victoria, local councils were debating the merits of throwing more funding at public libraries given their perceived loss of relevance and bleak outlook. In all respects, the industry was in need of strategic transformation.

Background

The previous year, the Victorian State Government, providers of approximately 20 per cent of library funding, had reduced its recurrent support to Victoria's 300-plus library services. This unexpected move was eventually overturned thanks to the concerted campaign Save Our Libraries. As the state government was to discover, threatening the future of public libraries was the equivalent of shooting Bambi's mother.

Nevertheless, the writing was on the wall. Public libraries, in their current format, were slowly being squeezed by social change. Attempts to respond to this changing world lacked cohesion and direction, reflecting the fact that at their core, public libraries were suffering from an identity crisis. In 2012, Victorian public libraries were no longer sure what they were, what they could be or what they should do.

The time had come for public libraries to stake their strategic position in the twenty-first century.

The purpose of this project was to develop a strategic framework for Victorian public libraries that would be applicable to a wide range of public library services (metropolitan, regional and rural) to guide their own strategic planning and to be meaningful at a local and state level. Development of the framework was a collaborative, industry-wide process involving more than 80 public library employees and stakeholders from across Victoria.

The near 20-year horizon recognised the need for a compelling long-term, industry-wide vision, and the uncertainty of planning for such a horizon naturally leant itself to the use of scenarios. Subsequently two scenarios for 2030 were created, from which transformational strategic positions for public libraries were identified and the necessary strategic objectives outlined. The recommendations in this strategic framework continue to guide the strategic direction and evolution of Victoria's public library sector today (see chapter 12).

Scenarios for 2030

Working across two days, and collaborating within teams, industry stakeholders created two scenarios for 2030 depicting the different environments in which public libraries may have to operate in the future. These were called the *Creative Scenario* and the *Community Scenario*.

The creative scenario describes the emergence of a post-materialistic culture and the associated shift away from material consumption. The drive for economic growth has been softened by broader measures of social progress, including personal time and mental health. And we see an increasing willingness to collaborate, particularly in the domains of consumption and creativity.

This scenario is defined by a growing interest in creativity as people seek to develop, express and share their creativity through writing, music, dance, multimedia, drawing, painting and theatre. In essence, the desire to create has emerged as a prominent social theme in 2030.

In the community scenario the needs for people to relearn, reskill and reconnect emerge as prominent community features in 2030. It's a scenario in which the dynamic nature of change demands a dynamic approach to learning. And being 'twenty-first-century literate' requires people to remain in a perpetual state of *learning, unlearning and relearning* to ensure their knowledge and skills remain relevant.

In this scenario, individual entrepreneurship, globalisation and technology have combined to cause political and industry fragmentation, contributing to the growing irrelevance of traditional gatekeepers. This disruption leads to sustained high unemployment and a growing sense of social displacement as knowledge and skills that have served for years become increasingly redundant ('Where do I fit in?'). With deepening distrust of large organisations (government, corporations, media), we see an increasing desire to reconnect with one's local community.

Broadening strategic identity

Historically, public libraries have served the purpose of *providing universal access to information*, a mission dating back to a time when access to information was relatively scarce. In this instance, the word *access* is limiting because it ties the relevance of public libraries to the continuing scarcity of access. But what happens when access to information is no longer a social scarcity? If public libraries persisted with this limiting sense of identity, they were at risk of losing further relevance, constrained by a narrow and outdated purpose that restricted them to incremental developments such as free access to other forms of media — the internet, DVDs, CDs and the like.

Clearly, the identity of public libraries needed to be broadened to enable future transformation. Providing access to information serves only a subset of society's broader information needs; the expanded purpose of *providing solutions to society's information needs* offers far greater flexibility to adjust services as information needs change over time while remaining true to the heritage of public libraries. With this broader strategic identity, public libraries take a major step towards perpetual relevance by effectively saying, 'We are here to help solve society's information needs no matter what they might be.' So what could these information needs be in 2030?

Analysing the 2030 scenarios

One week before the strategic positioning workshop in which attendees would design strategic responses to their 2030 scenarios, participants received their scenario narrative as a pre-read and were encouraged to place themselves in the future as they gave consideration to the following questions:

- Which scenario *themes*, features or needs are particularly relevant for the future of public libraries?
- What are the key *challenges* your scenario presents for public libraries?
- What are the key *opportunities* your scenario presents for public libraries?

These questions were then revisited during the workshop, when all team members shared their insights in a group setting, which allowed for a shared understanding to emerge and be captured.

The significant themes that emerged across the two scenarios with greatest relevance to Victorian public libraries were *creativity, collaboration, brain health, dynamic learning* and *community connection* (see figure 11.4). Note that the theme of brain health was significant in both scenarios, driven in part by the predetermined factor of an ageing population.

Creative Scenario			Community Scenario	
Creativity	**Collaboration**	**Brain Health**	**Dynamic Learning**	**Community Connection**
The desire to unlock, express, develop and record creative interests	The willingness to partner, co-operate and share with others	The need for lifelong mental engagement, stimulation and care	The need to continually learn new knowledge and skills to participate fully in a rapidly changing environment	The desire for stable and trusted relationships with people and places of common interest

Figure 11.4: 2030 scenario themes

These themes were then linked to future strategic opportunities for public libraries via the concepts of *functionality* and *content* or, more particularly, a *content spectrum* (showing the range of activities associated with content). This spectrum appears in figure 11.5, showing (from left to right) the creation of content, the management of content and the consumption of content by the end user.

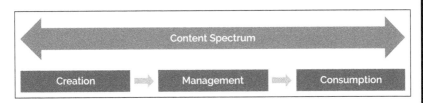

Figure 11.5: content spectrum

Given the traditional function of libraries as content managers, use of a content spectrum provided the essential link between the significant scenario themes and opportunities for future strategic positioning.

Public libraries had largely fulfilled their traditional purpose of providing universal access to information via a content management and distribution role. However, technology, higher education levels and increased personal wealth had reduced society's needs for such a service. So future strategic options for public libraries were explored by broadening their historical role in different directions along the content spectrum.

In the creative scenario, the rise of a creative culture moved the social need to the left end of the content spectrum towards *creation*. The unmet information need in this scenario is around creativity, as more and more people seek the skills and resources to develop and express their creativity ('Help us to create'). Hence the strategic opportunity for public libraries is to facilitate creativity and collaboration by evolving towards becoming the *creative library* — see figure 11.6 (i).

In the community scenario, we see the increasing need for dynamic learning and community connection. The rising social needs in this scenario lie to the right end of the content spectrum, around *how information is consumed*. As opposed to the largely informal learning that takes place today, public libraries in this scenario provide formal community learning spaces and programs. Here the strategic opportunity is to become the *community library*, providing the classes, workshops and spaces that support twenty-first-century literacy — see figure 11.6 (ii).

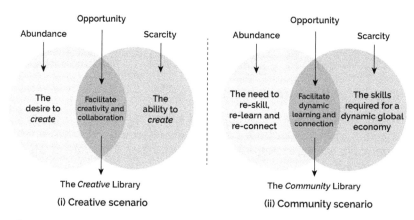

(i) Creative scenario

(ii) Community scenario

Figure 11.6: strategic opportunity identification

Strategic opportunities were identified in both scenarios by expanding the strategic identity of public libraries to providing solutions to society's information needs.

Strategic vision

The following questions proved an effective combination in helping participants to generate a future strategic vision from their scenario analysis:

- What *functions or roles* could a relevant and successful public library perform in this scenario?
- In essence, what type of role would a public library perform in 2030?

Articulating the different functions or roles a public library could perform in 2030 produced numerous varied responses as participants outlined future opportunities. Output from groups who worked on the creative library vision included:

- a recording studio for film and music
- more creative programs
- open 24/7
- part of a cultural and arts precinct
- more community engagement areas
- soundproof booths
- a place that provides information technology equipment
- a catalyst for creativity
- a more prominent creative art space
- a place where people go to learn new skills
- a vibrant place where new thinking emerges
- a community centre.

The follow-up question asks participants to summarise the general theme running through these functions and to express it in a succinct vision ('In essence, we will be ... '). In the creative scenario, where the primary role of the public library broadens to facilitating creative development and expression in a collaborative environment, the aspirational *vision* for the creative library is:

to become the community's central hub for creative development and expression.

In fulfilling this role, public libraries provide the products, services, programs, facilities and support that enables the community to unlock, express, develop, record and share their creative interests and output.

In the community scenario, the primary role of the public library broadens to become the community's hub for dynamic learning and social connection. The aspirational *vision* for the community library is:

to become the community agora — the people's place.

In this role, the focus of a public library is on learning delivery — *how information and knowledge are consumed*. And in fulfilling their role as a hub for community learning and social connection, public libraries provide the products, services, programs, facilities and support that enable the community to reskill, relearn and reconnect.

Both of these strategic visions presented opportunities for public libraries to continue their transition from passive, product-based environments, to delivering dynamic, service-based experiences (see figure 11.7). More importantly, these strategic positions clarified the *types* of active service experiences public libraries could provide in the future — servicing their community's information and learning needs with regard to creativity and twenty-first-century literacy — while expanding their role to satisfy broader community needs for collaboration and belonging.

Creative
Library

Public Libraries: Customer Experience

Passive, product-based   Active, service-based

Community
Library

Figure 11.7: evolution of public library services

The creative and community library options are complementary strategic directions that can be pursued simultaneously by Victorian public libraries according to local wants and needs.

Just as the world in 2030 is likely to include elements from both scenarios, so too will Victorian public libraries evolve to become a blend of the creative library and the community library, with the specific relevance of each strategic option varying according to local community wants and needs. Importantly, these different strategic options can be pursued simultaneously, and are complementary to the traditional content management and distribution role played by public libraries.

Typically, of course, any strategic framework includes only a single vision, but this was an industry-wide framework intended to *guide* the future direction of public libraries, rather than being too prescriptive, so the decision was made to keep the two separate visions to provide greater differentiation in the choices facing Victorian public libraries.

As the product of a scenarios exercise, a compelling vision is effectively a 'complexity reducer'[8]. If scenarios with their multiple futures and uncertainty introduce complexity, then the strategic positioning that results from these scenarios represents the simplicity on the other side. Consequently, library managers emerged from the VPL2030 process with a renewed sense of clarity around what libraries were, where they were headed and what they could do (see figure 11.8, overleaf).

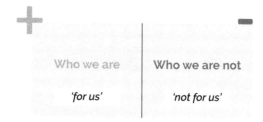

Figure 11.8: strategic clarity

Strategic positioning informed by scenarios provides an empowering sense of clarity around where the organisation is headed and the scope of activities that are 'for us' or 'not for us'.

Strategic objectives

Bringing a vision to life begins with identifying the broad domains essential to success — where do we need to focus to achieve our goals? Strategic objectives are then outlined articulating what it is we're trying to achieve in each domain that is consistent with our strategic vision.

Completing the 2030 strategic framework were five strategic objectives to support the future vision for public libraries as dynamic, service-based facilities (see table 11.1). As with any long-term framework, these objectives were necessarily broad, directing focus to areas for prioritisation, but leaving the execution (what to do, how to do it, when to do it) open to local interpretation. These objectives are robust since they can be equally effective no matter which scenario develops. And they allow flexibility for individual public libraries to evolve towards providing creative and/or community library offerings depending on the strength of emerging community wants and needs.

Table 11.1: strategic objectives

Strategic domains	Strategic objectives
Storytelling	To generate internal and external belief and buy-in to a shared vision for the future role of Victorian public libraries

Revenue and funding	To develop a portfolio of revenue and funding streams that ensure the future prosperity of Victorian public libraries
Products, services and programs	To offer a suite of products, services and programs that meet the community's changing expectations and needs of a public library into the future • To offer a suite of products, services and programs that meet the community's expectations and needs for creative development, expression and collaboration (*creative library*) • To offer a suite of products, services and programs that meet the community's expectations and needs for dynamic learning and social connection (*community library*)
Facilities and resources	To incorporate a mix of flexible spaces that facilitate and support the range of public library products and services into the future • To incorporate a mix of flexible spaces that facilitate and support an environment of creativity and collaboration (*creative library*) • To incorporate a mix of flexible spaces that facilitate and support an environment of community learning and social connection (*community library*)
Staff	To develop a flexible and inclusive culture that attracts and retains people with the right skills and attitude to deliver public library products and services into the future

Assessing strategies against scenarios

One of the enduring misunderstandings about scenario planning concerns how to design strategies in response to multiple scenarios. Do we create a different strategy for each scenario? The answer is yes and no. In a workshop setting, individual groups develop strategic responses to their particular scenarios. However, each of these responses is not then developed to the point where the organisation has four fully polished, off-the-shelf strategies to choose from — remember, the time for complexity created by multiple choices is over. We are now working towards a single strategic vision.

Instead, the individual strategies are assessed against all scenarios and the output synthesised to produce a single optimal strategy that supports the corporate vision and is resilient across the scenarios. Note that we are aiming for the *optimal* strategy across the scenarios, not the safest. This is an exercise in entrepreneurialism, not mediocrity.

In this context, building resilience into your strategy does not have a defensive or cautious connotation; rather, it means supporting your core strategy with the contingency or complementary opportunities presented by the scenarios. For example, the shift by Toyota to in-home mobility solutions and robotics ensures a more resilient organisation in an uncertain environment. This is not a defensive move; it's a logical offensive step that optimises use of its internal capabilities and diversifies its revenue sources.

The key point here is that an optimal strategy and a resilient strategy are not mutually exclusive; they are complementary. You optimise a strategy by building resilience into it.

An effective technique for assessing the viability of future strategies against the scenarios is to categorise each according to the following criteria[9]:

- 'no painers'—strategies that hold well under some scenarios and are indifferent in others
- 'no brainers'—strategies that hold well under all scenarios
- 'big gains / big pains'—strategies that hold well under some scenarios but may be adverse under others
- 'no gainers'—strategies that are ill-advised under all scenarios.

When building an optimal and resilient strategy, where your core strategy or product appears in the contingent domain (see figure 11.9), meaning there are some scenarios in which it doesn't prosper, your task is to extend your capabilities into relevant opportunity areas that do prosper in these scenarios. At the same time, how do you modify your core business to maintain prosperity in these scenarios? The purpose at all times is to build organisational resilience through a diverse and flexible strategy that optimises returns from internal capabilities in a turbulent and uncertain environment.

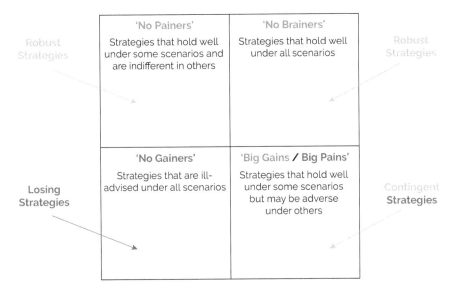

Figure 11.9: strategy viability matrix

Organisational resilience relies on a diverse and flexible strategy that optimises returns from internal capabilities in a turbulent and uncertain environment.

Strategic creativity and originality

In the transformational findings and recommendations of the VPL2030 strategic framework, we see the impact of the powerful entrepreneurial combination of scenarios and a broad sense of strategic identity. Working hand-in-hand, this combination enabled industry stakeholders to transcend incrementalism, empowering them to create original strategic positions that were relevant to the future learning and information needs of their communities.

The vast potential for public libraries to play a central role within their community is why *storytelling* is perhaps the most important of the five strategic objectives contained within the framework. The 2030 scenarios and strategic visions have armed the industry with a positive and relevant story to tell—one that is critical to transforming the outdated public and political perceptions of libraries as solely about books.

As this story is told, it will become more and more apparent how short-sighted my cynical friends were when they forecast that libraries won't exist in the future. Although physical books *may* play a less prominent role in the future, the 2030 scenarios have shown that public libraries might be more relevant than ever.

CHAPTER 12

'Now what?' — Transitioning to the future

Integration with internal processes is essential to scenario relevance and organisational action

This chapter is dedicated to the memory of John Murrell, who sadly passed away in June 2016. John was President of the Public Libraries Victoria Network from 2009 to 2016 and was much loved by the Victorian public library community, for whom he has created a lasting legacy.

John Murrell (right) and myself at the launch of the Victorian Public Libraries 2030 Strategic Framework, June 2013

I first met John Murrell in April 2012 during the interview phase of the Victorian Public Libraries 2030 project. A quietly spoken and unassuming man, John made an instant impression with his thoughts on the possible futures of public libraries. It was John who introduced me to the concept of recording studios in Scandinavian public libraries I mentioned in chapter 8. As President of the Public Libraries Victoria Network (PLVN), the peak body for Victoria's public library sector and a co-sponsor of the project, John was respected throughout the industry and was a leader who influenced through collaboration.

While he was a significant contributor throughout the project, it was during the execution phase of the strategic framework that John's leadership qualities came to the fore as an internal driving force behind implementation of the framework's recommendations. In developing and assessing industry project initiatives, John would insist that the framework was used as a constant reference point, ensuring that Victorian public libraries were taking a consistent and coherent approach to the future, and that any projects supported the long-term vision for public libraries. As a consequence, the VPL2030 strategic framework underpinned all PLVN planning and project development from the time of its launch.[1]

The implementation leadership shown by John and his executive team at PLVN helped to set a cultural standard for strategic planning that runs throughout the public library sector, and in 2018 the framework continued to be used as a constant source of reference and guidance, both externally ('Are our assumptions about future societal developments still valid?') and internally ('What initiatives should be prioritised and funded?').

To step inside a Victorian public library today is to see the unfolding strategic visions for 2030 come to life: language classes and digital literacy workshops; accredited courses, innovations labs and entrepreneurial co-working spaces; art classes and youth engagement programs; recording studios and editing facilities; recreational groups using the library as a meeting space, and vibrant cafés offering the opportunity for people to gather and connect.

In my experience, no industry or organisation has made better use of a scenarios-based strategic framework than the Victorian public library sector. Their constant reference back to the framework as a guide for strategic direction, prioritisation and implementation has been exemplary and provides a benchmark for other industries and organisations to follow.

The success of this implementation demonstrates, in particular, the power and importance of an internal driving force—someone to pick up the baton and turn a theoretical strategic framework into practical outcomes. Such an advocate is most important when there is no formal plan to support implementation of the broader strategic framework, as was the case in this instance. Ideally you want both.

Without either an influential internal advocate or a shorter-term implementation plan, any strategic framework will always struggle to make an organisational impact—a point that became obvious to me over the course of subsequent projects.

Back to earth

Buoyed by the success of the Victorian public libraries project, I thought I had cracked the code to linking scenarios to organisational impact: a long-term strategic framework with a compelling corporate vision supported by relevant strategic objectives was the essential output for driving organisational action. Or so I thought.

Over the next couple of years, I undertook two other major projects where the intention was to design long-term frameworks to guide the client's future strategic direction. Both of these projects had goals, processes, timelines and participation similar to those of the VPL2030 project, including:

- positioning the clients for sustained future success
- 12-month projects with 10-year scenario horizons
- 20-plus senior managers involved.

In one project the client was a large multinational firm; in the other, a group of industry leaders looking to co-design a strategic framework to guide their individual businesses. The impact with both of these clients was not nearly as great. This had nothing to do with the quality of the scenarios, which continued to be legitimate references for decision making. Nor were the strategic positioning or strategic objective recommendations any less substantial. Still, *something* was missing.

What this 'something' was exactly was made all too clear to me when I checked in on the participants from the second, industry-wide project, 12 months later. When I asked for a show of hands from the executives to indicate those who had taken action relating to the framework, only two participants responded positively, one of whom seemed a little hesitant. As for the others? Nothing. Just a wall of silence and what seemed like the deliberate avoidance of eye contact.

The reason for this lack of action became apparent during the lunch break when I overheard the comment, 'It's just too vague; how can you act on it?' It seemed I was back in the world of scenario ineffectiveness. While I had taken a step forward from 'what's next?' to address the client's 'so what?' challenge, there was still another important step missing. I hadn't addressed the final managerial concern—namely, 'Now what do we do with it?'

Without an internal driving force to carry the work forward, the strategic framework, which had been the result of an eight-month collaboration, remained on the shelf for these senior executives. What was missing was a shorter-term strategic plan to give operational meaning to the framework and provide a direct line of sight between the longer-term outlook and the organisation's more immediate priorities, something to drive action and introduce accountability.

Linking the strategic framework to organisational action

The strategic plan takes the earliest period of the strategic framework and fleshes it out with specific details, including:

- **strategies, objectives and actions**—to support the strategic framework
- **responsibilities**—which individuals or business units will do what?
- **timings**—when will the actions be completed?

In doing so, the shorter-term plan achieves several purposes:

- **Integration.** The strategic plan completes the integration of the scenarios with the organisation's established planning and operations processes. This integration is achieved via the strategic domains and objectives from the long-term strategic framework, which are then used to drive development of the shorter-term plan (see figure 12.3, page 249). This linkage provides a direct line of sight between the scenarios and the organisation's day-to-day operations and priorities.
- **Alignment.** The strategic plan ensures business unit activities align with broader corporate direction and goals.
- **Impact.** The strategic plan introduces accountability for impact by including *responsibility* and *timing* for actions. These inclusions clarify expectations and accountability, and visibly link individual and business unit performance appraisal with organisational priorities.
- **Efficiency.** The strategic plan ensures cohesive and efficient organisational transition. Developed within the broader context of a strategic framework, strategic plans effectively take on the role of transitional strategies, introducing a series of *innovation segues* to cohesively transition the organisation towards its future vision.

CASE STUDY

Melton City Council, 2017–18

In chapter 10 I provide extensive detail on how to build scenarios using a project with Melton City Council as a case study to illustrate my process. Development of these scenarios represented phase one of what was in fact a comprehensive three-phase strategy process, with phase two producing a long-term corporate strategy in response to the scenarios (strategic framework) and phase three being development of a four-year implementation plan to drive action (see figure 12.1).

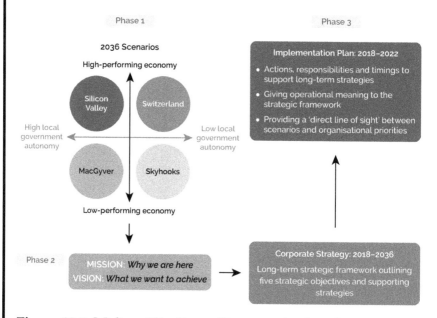

Figure 12.1: Melton City Council's strategic planning process

Informed by long-term scenarios, Melton City Council's corporate strategy and supporting implementation plan represents an exemplary end-to-end strategy process.

Both the corporate strategy and the supporting implementation plan were developed within one-day workshop settings in which participants collaborated in teams—with one major difference. In the second workshop on strategic positioning, where the goal was to assess and develop strategic responses to the four scenarios, participants worked within the same diverse teams as they did in the original scenarios workshop. This consistency is logical since the frame of reference for decision making is the *external* scenarios. In the third workshop, focusing on implementation, the frame of reference for decision making shifts to the *internal* strategic objectives and strategies, and the purpose is to develop actions that support these objectives. In this workshop participants worked within their business unit teams.

In the strategic positioning workshop, individual groups defined the organisation's mission and vision for their scenario before outlining the strategic domains and objectives necessary to achieve their vision. Each group then added a layer of depth to the corporate strategy by also outlining the strategic priorities and objectives necessary to achieve their broad strategic objectives. Given the nature of the planning horizon, these supporting priorities remained relatively broad in nature while providing a greater level of detail to improve the usefulness of the corporate strategy. These strategic priorities and objectives then provided the essential link between the longer-term corporate strategy and the forthcoming implementation plan. Output from this workshop was captured in the template in figure 12.2 (overleaf).

At the conclusion of the strategic positioning workshop, the output of the four teams was synthesised into a long-term corporate strategy consisting of a corporate mission and vision, five strategic domains and objectives and 20 supporting strategies. All participants were actively involved in the synthesising process, maintaining the emphasis on participant buy-in. The corporate strategy was then distributed to all participants one week prior to the third and final workshop as a pre-read.

Strategic domain: _____

Strategic objective:

Strategies	Objectives
Strategic priority 1	Objective 1
Strategic priority 2	Objective 2
Strategic priority 3	Objective 3
Strategic priority 4	Objective 4

Figure 12.2: fleshing out the corporate strategy

Strategic priorities outline the focus areas essential to achieving strategic objectives, providing a level of depth to the corporate strategy that improves its organisational usefulness.

The purpose of the implementation planning workshop was to give operational meaning to the corporate strategy by outlining the relevant actions to be undertaken by individual business units. Working within their operational teams, business units were challenged to assess how they could *make a difference* to achieving the objectives outlined in the corporate strategy. Such a process ensures the relevance of the implementation plan throughout the organisation, thereby improving the practical relevance of both the corporate strategy and the scenarios.

To ensure thinking remained at a strategic level, participants were advised against trying to be too specific in their responses and to capture only the significant actions that could *make a difference* to achieving the strategies and objectives. Still, a total of 135 possible actions were generated during the workshop. Overlap between some of the group's actions and the folding of lower-order actions into higher-order outcomes meant that this number was eventually trimmed to a final plan comprising 65 actions. Output from this workshop was captured in the template in figure 12.3.

Strategic domain: _____

Strategic objective:		Strategic priorities provide the essential link to the corporate strategy	
Strategies	**Actions**	**Responsibilities**	**Timing**
Strategic priority 1 ◄ Objective 1	•	Manager A	Year 1
	•	Manager B	Year 2
Strategic priority 2 ◄ Objective 2	•	Manager C	Year 4
	•	Manager A	Year 2

Figure 12.3: linking the long-term plan to organisational action

Strategic priorities are the essential link between the long-term corporate strategy and the implementation plan.

To complete the loop on what is an exemplary end-to-end process, a reporting framework was established requiring managers to update Council's executive on implementation progress at half-yearly intervals. Such a framework ensures internal accountability and alignment and completes the integration of the scenarios with the organisation's processes and operations.

CHAPTER 13

Making sense of the patterns in the chaos

Scenarios provide the essential context for anticipating the future

'You've called women you don't like fat pigs, dogs, slobs and disgusting animals ...,' began Fox News moderator Megyn Kelly during the first televised debate among Republican candidates at the start of their primary campaign in August 2015.

'Only Rosie O'Donnell,' Donald Trump interrupted deadpan.

And with that remark, the rules for the 2016 US presidential election were thrown out the window.

As I watched the debate on 6 August 2015, it was clear that Donald Trump was on a winner, that he *was* the 'event' to give voice to the latent political disaffection of millions of US voters.

On stage with nine other candidates representing 'politics as usual', Trump stood out like a beacon as his opponents delivered contrived, scripted responses, rolling out what they thought the public wanted to hear. Yet these men succeeded only in demonstrating a tin ear with regard to the public's mood for political change. Against this backdrop, Trump dominated the debate. He dominated the stage, and the subsequent headlines.

On the Democratic side, a similar phenomenon was occurring. As soon as you knew anything about Bernie Sanders or his political views you knew he was a genuine candidate who was in it for the long haul. The fact that he described himself as a Democratic Socialist, a label that was anathema to much of the US media, was irrelevant. The people wanted authenticity. They wanted conviction. And most of all they wanted change.

For millions of voters, politics was no longer a party or policy issue so much as a process issue. For these people, the system was broken and rigged, and no political 'insider' was going to fix it. What was needed was a person or personality from *outside the system*. Which explains how two candidates who appeared miles apart from a policy perspective were attracting voters for the same basic reason: 'We've had enough!'

The US primary voting season of 2015–16 has been described as 'unprecedented', and as producing 'unimaginable' outcomes. So why did so many so-called political experts continue to underestimate the rise of Donald Trump or dismiss the appeal of Bernie Sanders throughout their campaigns? Because they lacked a context for interpreting or understanding what was happening. Their only reference was the past, and according to the past:

- establishment politics always triumphs
- successful candidates behave in a *presidential* manner
- media spend determines election results
- political experience is always a strength.

But in 2015 these 'rules' no longer applied, and the political class and the parties themselves were exposed by the novelty of the situation they in fact had helped to create. And without a reference point for anticipating, interpreting or responding to unfolding events, the political establishment continued to misread, underestimate and respond inappropriately to circumstances for which they were unprepared.

Having taken only a passing interest in previous US primary elections, I was particularly sensitive to this campaign because its developments were so timely. The previous month I had completed a set of scenarios that explored the themes of a grassroots political backlash and the seemingly insatiable thirst for entertainment caused by shortening attention spans. In the *backlash scenario*, disillusionment with politics as usual, the rise of community-driven decision making and a movement away from the traditional political parties were the dominant themes. In the *attention scenario*, an 'entertainment at all costs' paradigm intruded on every aspect of life (politics, sport and so on) and life itself became the ultimate 'reality show'.

In presenting the *political scenario*, I made the point that the mood of the Australian electorate could be summed up by the famous line from the 1976 film *Network*: 'I'm as mad as hell, and I'm not going to take this anymore!'[1] And why shouldn't it be? Over the previous decade respect for the political system had degenerated to the point where massive electoral 'blowback' was only a matter of time:

- The major parties' policy positions had converged—'They're all the same!'
- Political communication had been reduced to clichés and slogans that meant little and seemed to assume the public were stupid—'Going for growth ... moving forward'
- Politicians were increasingly being stage-managed and isolated from the general public to avoid potential embarrassment. (Bizarre incidents such as Australian Prime Minister Tony Abbott casually eating a raw onion on national television as he strolled through a Tasmanian produce farm, and British Prime Minister David Cameron eating a hotdog with a knife and fork during the 2015 election campaign at an 'average family' barbecue come to mind.)
- And politicians demonstrated little understanding of local issues and concerns as they became bogged down in myopic political in-fighting and point scoring—'They're out of touch!'

Given these developments, it was little wonder that people had become disengaged from politics ('Why bother?'). However, I made the point that disengagement should not be confused with indifference. In fact, these circumstances created fertile ground where minor parties and independents could emerge, capitalising on the passion and discontent of the general public.

This scenario was particularly important to my client because the prosperity of their core product relied to a large degree on the maintenance of establishment politics. Yet if events in the US were to be repeated in Australia in the following year's federal election, then the protection afforded by the political status quo could well disappear, in which case my client's challenge would no longer be about market share, but about market size. So the political scenario was designed as an impetus to act, a catalyst to continue diversifying their business *ahead of time*.

Primed for the future

In her classic study of the intelligence failures surrounding the Pearl Harbor attack, historian Roberta Wohlstetter writes,

It is much easier after the event to sort the relevant from the irrelevant signals. After the event, of course, a signal is always crystal clear; we can now see what disaster it was signalling, since the disaster has occurred. But before the event it is obscure and pregnant with conflicting meanings. It comes to the observer embedded in an atmosphere of 'noise', i.e. in the company of all sorts of information that is useless and irrelevant for predicting the particular disaster.

'To discriminate significant sounds against this background of noise,' she explains, 'one has to be listening for something or for one of several things. In short, one needs not only an ear, but a variety of hypotheses that guide observation.'[2]

The result of the 2016 US presidential election demonstrates the ongoing value of scenarios as a primer for the future. They provide the necessary future context (Wohlstetter's *hypotheses*) for anticipating, interpreting and responding to events. Our scenarios didn't predict the election of Donald Trump, but they did increase our sensitivity to his emergence. From thousands of kilometres away, my client's management team were able to detect relevance in, and make sense of, 'unprecedented' events unfolding in the US primaries, and then derive meaning for their own business operations in Australia.

Their competitors, meanwhile, did not enjoy the same advantage. They were unlikely to draw any connection between anti-establishment sentiment among US voters, the rise of Donald Trump and any existential threat to their industry in Australia. How could they? They had no hypotheses for making such a connection.

Context in any situation provides grounds for understanding. Think about the first time you were exposed to a foreign sport, be it American gridiron, Irish hurling or the traditional sport of buzkashi in Afghanistan. To the untrained eye, these games seem like a jumble of random, seemingly unrelated actions, lacking any evidence of organised method. Yet each sport is highly strategic and systematic. In the absence of any context for understanding the game as it unfolds before you, all you see is randomness. It's the same with the future.

To detect and understand the meaning of subtle changes as they occur, you need to be sensitive to their future contextual significance. For this you need to develop a corporate 'future memory'.

Developing a corporate memory of the future

In 1985 the journal *Human Neurobiology* published a paper by leading Swedish brain psychologist David Ingvar[3] that had major implications for business strategy, and scenario planners in particular consider its publication a landmark. Some of its key findings can be summarised like this:

- People have different memory systems: memories of the past and *memories of the future.*

- We create memories of the future by visualising pathways forward to desired or anticipated outcomes (future scenarios). These scenarios can be described in detail even though they are yet to occur. At the simplest level, consider your plans for the weekend:
  - What will you be doing?
  - Who will you be spending time with?
  - Where do you have to be at certain times?
  - How will you get there?
- Our memories of the future act as a sort of filter to prevent our being overwhelmed by information. Random information that does not *fit* with our memories of the future tends to be ignored or actively filtered out. On the other hand, information that does fit with our memories of the future may be perceived and experienced as significant, and acted upon accordingly.

  We experience this effect when we are in the market for a new car and suddenly notice just how many car yards there are on our daily route to work.

- Information is filtered according to its perceived relevance to our memories of the future — our expectations, goals and plans.
- Only by accessing our memory of the future can we detect and perceive meaning from amongst the constant volley of signals to which we are constantly exposed.

'The message from this research is clear,' suggests Arie de Geus.

We will not perceive a signal from the outside world unless it is relevant to an option for the future that we have already worked out in our imaginations. The more "memories of the future" we develop, the more open and receptive we will be to signals from the outside world.[4]

Two conclusions for companies and for strategic design are significant:

- Organisations with narrow or underdeveloped memories of the future (scenarios, strategic reasoning) will always struggle to anticipate significant changes in their business environment or to make sense of signals before it's too late. For these companies, important changes on the fringe will always sit outside their sphere of attention and perception.

- In times of uncertainty and turbulence, organisations should develop an 'arsenal' of future memories[5]—a store of future scenarios and pathways of signals to each of these futures.

Anticipating the future

I first met Damian Farrow in 2008 when I was researching the perception skills of champion athletes and how this might relate to organisational foresight. Damian was working with elite athletes at the Australian Institute of Sport, studying and teaching perception, and his findings seemed to have some important insights for business.

Farrow's interest in perception and anticipation had begun when he was a competitive tennis player. Frustrated by a lack of speed, and noticing that top tennis players could predict the direction and speed of the ball before it left their opponent's racquet, Farrow asked: *'What is it these experts intuitively see that the rest of us don't? What cues are they picking up on, and when?'*[6]

His process and findings are described in the following excerpt from the *Wired* article *Wayne Gretzky-Style 'Field Sense' May Be Teachable:*[7]

To understand what experts were seeing, Farrow meticulously dismantled the mechanics of the serve. He recruited two groups of players—novices and experts—and outfitted each with earmuffs and occlusion goggles, clear glasses that turn opaque when an assistant on the sidelines flips an electronic switch. He then put the athletes on court opposite an expert server. As the server's arm went back for the shot, Farrow would black out the goggles, leaving players to swing blindly at the incoming ball.

The point of the exercise was to identify exactly when a seasoned player knew where the ball would head. Farrow established five possible windows: First, he blackened the goggles just as the ball's flight path over the net was determined; second, as

the server's racket made contact with the ball. Then he gave players less and less information—cutting off the image when the server's arm was cocked, as it was being drawn back, and, finally, at the very start of the toss.

Not surprisingly, receivers were better at guessing the ball's direction the later their vision cut out. But the results also revealed something more interesting. Graphs of the amateurs' reactions showed that they could anticipate where the ball would go only if they witnessed the racket making contact with it. Experts knew what would happen roughly a third of a second earlier, when the server's cocked arm was still unfolding.

What happened in that fraction of a second? A lot, Farrow reasoned. Up to a point, he theorized, the direction of a serve was fundamentally unpredictable: Whatever clues existed weren't ones that an opposing player could discern. By the time the ball had been hit, on the other hand, even a novice could make a plausible guess at its trajectory.

What separated the pros from everyone else was the ability to pull directional information out of the early stages of a swing and therefore to predict a split second earlier where to head.

This fraction of time is game-changing. A serve going 120 miles per hour takes approximately a third of a second to travel the 60 feet from baseline to service line. This means that an expert, who doesn't have to wait until contact, has twice as long to move, plant his feet, and swing.

This discovery fit with something Farrow and other tennis researchers had already suspected: Reflex speed is not the key factor in returning a serve. "People have tested casual players and experts, and their reaction times are essentially the same," Farrow says. The fact that Roger Federer can drill back a 140-mile-per-hour serve is partly a matter of muscle control. But it's also about processing subtle visual cues to predict where the ball will go and get to the right spot.

The analogy between processing cues from a serve in tennis and detecting significance in early signals of change in the business environment is obvious. I noted in chapter 1 that one of the problems with relying on obvious trends is that your competitors will also be aware of them, thus limiting any advantage you might gain. To borrow from Farrow's research, 'by the time the ball had been hit, even a novice could make a plausible guess at its trajectory'.

On the other hand, just as an expert tennis player can process subtle cues to predict where the ball will go and get to the right spot, so too can corporations develop the sensitivity to detect, process and respond to weak signals of change. Scenarios and backcasting hold the key to developing this sensitivity.

Increasing sensitivity to change

In chapter 10 I talk about how backcasting is a process that works back from your end scenarios to show how they could develop. This method is not only effective for demonstrating scenario plausibility, it also plays a significant role in helping to make sense of future change. Just as Damian Farrow meticulously dismantled the mechanics of the serve to understand what experts were seeing, backcasting effectively dismantles your end scenarios, breaking them down into earlier iterations through a two-step process:

1. identifying key features of your scenarios that are significant for your strategic challenge

   (What are the differences that make a difference?)

2. identifying factors or events that could enable these significant scenario outcomes to develop

   (What does the development of each scenario rely on?)

These are the *subtle cues* referred to in Farrow's article. Backcasting provides a framework for ongoing scanning by identifying precursor events (cues), which provide signposts to the development of your end scenarios. The strategic benefit of this framework is a corporate intelligence for anticipating and interpreting change—managers are now equipped with a future memory of signals to scan for.

Examples of the types of signals scanners should be sensitive to are *perception-shaping events, behaviour-enabling events* and *emerging behaviour signals*.

PERCEPTION-SHAPING EVENTS[8]

These events help to shape society's perceptions, from one belief to another. Often the events are extreme, thus capturing the public's attention and penetrating their established views. Examples include the Three Mile Island nuclear accident in 1979; Hurricane Katrina and periods of severe drought and deadly bushfires in California, which have affected attitudes on climate change; and the 2008 global financial crisis, which influenced social attitudes towards rampant materialism.

For the environmental scanner, two questions in particular should guide their attention:

- What social perceptions and attitudes are significant within our scenarios?
- Which events might enable these perceptions and attitudes to be influential?

BEHAVIOUR-ENABLING EVENTS

These are events that enable behaviours significant to your scenarios to emerge. Examples include the rise of politicians or political parties promoting relevant policies; the building of necessary infrastructure (roads, bridges, airports, telecommunications); advancements in technology; or favourable economic conditions. As mentioned at the start of this chapter, the candidacies of Sanders and Trump were instantly recognised as significant behaviour-enabling events because they gave a voice to disengaged voters.

Again, the questions to guide ongoing scanning might include:

- Which behaviours are significant within our scenarios?
- Which events might enable these behaviours to emerge?

EMERGING BEHAVIOUR SIGNALS

These are confirming or disconfirming signals that indicate whether relevant behaviours are or are not emerging. These signals are often measurable changes, such as growth in telecommuting or rising participation in arts courses.

Interpreting the future

Detecting significance in otherwise random events requires a broad mindset to enable optimal sensitivity. The scenarios themselves describe a series of specific events to demonstrate the cause-and-effect logic of their story, but these events should not be taken literally. Rather, they are a means to an end and should be treated as such. It's the effects or outcomes of these events that matter for ongoing environmental scanning.

Given that multiple events are capable of producing the same outcome, managers should be sensitive to *any* event that might contribute to the outcomes relevant to their scenario. For example, the political scenario mentioned earlier did not explicitly mention a Trump or a Sanders, but it did describe the broad rejection of the political establishment. How this scenario develops is not as important as the development of the central theme itself.

With this scenario as a future memory, the sensing organisation might perceive any number of diverse signals as relevant to their hypotheses, such as:

- a scandal involving the misuse of taxpayer funds, which further erodes faith in the political system
- an exposé of the behind-the-scenes influence of faceless political lobbyists
- the rise of the sharing economy, which points to a growing emphasis on 'trust' in relationships.

Ongoing strategic monitoring

With your scenarios as a reference point for future developments, ongoing environmental scanning then serves two strategic purposes:

- **reviewing** — monitoring the external environment for signals that confirm or disconfirm development of the scenarios, or point to the emergence of altogether new futures

- **refreshing**—providing a link between your current strategy and your next round of strategy development via the collection of new information and insights, which feeds into the next series of scenario development.

Thus, the organisation has institutionalised environmental sensitivity as a strategic competency through a continuous loop of learning, creating, adapting and monitoring (see figure 13.1).

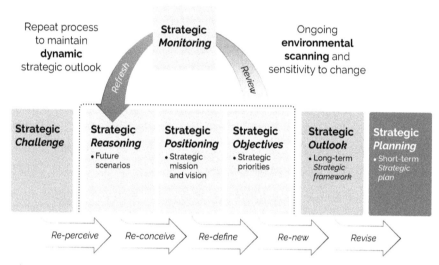

Figure 13.1: strategic monitoring

Ongoing scanning ensures organisational sensitivity to changes in the external environment and provides stimulus for the next round of strategic design.

So what's the benefit of this institutional sensitivity?

In effect, the organisation becomes a sensing animal, its employees alert to the subtle differences that make a difference. This outstanding strategic benefit is perfectly captured in the following excerpt from an interview between anthropologist Robbie Davis-Floyd and Betty Sue Flowers, writer of Shell's 1992 and 1995 scenarios[9]:

Robbie Davis-Floyd: When you talked about Shell as a largely decentralized corporation, I suddenly realized how powerful the stories [scenarios] must be at the ends of the... You know how if you diagram a corporation you go out to the individual units out there in the field where the action is, where it's most profoundly and immediately happening? If those individuals are the ones that are perceiving trends because of the stories, because of what they've been taught in the seminars, and then acting immediately, what you have overall is a corporate structure that really looks very much like an octopus with a brain in each arm.

Betty Sue Flowers: Yes, Shell is very fluid, very decentralized, so they can make quick responses on the ground, like one arm of the octopus reacting to a change. I think that's one reason for their success, and their longevity.

Internalising scenario proficiency

Let's say you're a middle-aged person who has let their health slip in recent years. Work, family and other commitments have made life busier and your own physical fitness has taken a backseat. One day you decide to do something about it by taking up running. On the first day you decide to run 2 kilometres. It's slow and painful, and it leaves you hopelessly out of breath. The effort takes 18 minutes. Still, you've done the best you can with the abilities you have at the time.

So you persist. A month later you're running 4 kilometres in 26 minutes. Once again, at the end of each run you're exhausted, having given everything you can. You're already running much further and faster. Encouraged by these results, you keep going. Three months pass and you're now running 6 kilometres in 27 minutes. The effort still leaves you gasping for breath, but your capabilities have improved significantly: you're now running three times your original distance at twice the speed. From this position, you look back and marvel at the results you're producing. You're now easily passing performance markers that once stretched you to breaking point.

It's the same with scenario planning. Through repeated application, the organisation builds its scenario learning capabilities and extends its consideration of plausible changes in the external environment. At the same time, managerial insight into what the organisation could be in the future also deepens (see figure 13.2, overleaf).

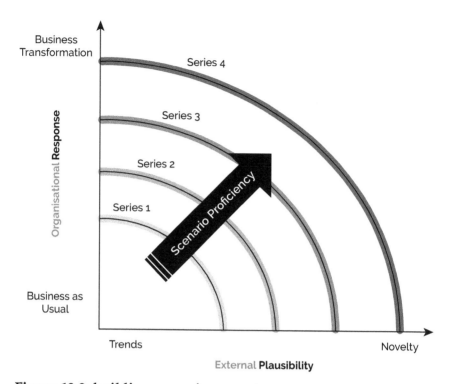

Figure 13.2: building scenario competency

As scenario competency builds with each exercise, the organisation extends its consideration of plausible external developments and possible strategic responses.

As familiarity with the process builds, participants will likely look back at earlier scenarios that were considered a stretch at the time and realise just how *safe* their thinking was, with the influence of obvious trends likely looming large. As competency builds, participants will naturally extend their understanding of what is plausible both externally and internally. External developments and internal responses that were previously dismissed or overlooked suddenly come into consideration as the firm becomes comfortable and competent in dealing with uncertainty, discontinuities and strategic transformation. With scenario planning, as with the novice runner, abilities and impact improve with persistence.

Embedding scenario proficiency delivers other strategic benefits in terms of (1) keeping managerial perceptions sharp and (2) expanding the organisation's strategic repertoire.

1. SHARPENING MANAGERIAL PERCEPTIONS

Given the fluidity of change, strategic outlooks need to be regularly refreshed to keep managerial perceptions sharp and organisational strategies in harmony with the environment. Externally, new forces are always emerging, other factors may be developing in ways that are different from what you expected, and embryonic issues are always lurking. Internally, organisational priorities can change over time, or new management can arrive with different perceptions of where the world is heading.

For these reasons, it's important for organisations to refresh their strategic scenarios every three to five years in sync with other internal planning commitments, thus providing a rolling long-term framework to guide shorter-term strategies and initiatives. Such a period allows enough time for new signals and issues to emerge. Regular scenario development also keeps managerial perceptions sharp, preventing intellectual complacency and the opening of any perception gap.

When previous scenarios remain relevant, the temptation can be to resist undertaking new iterations ('We don't need them — everything's on track'). Such an attitude falls for the illusion of market stability and misses the learning intention of scenarios. It's this learning that keeps managerial perceptions about the future sharp. In effect, the scenarios act as the organisation's sharpening stone, allowing you to constantly test and hone your perceptions and assumptions about the external environment.

2. EXPANDING YOUR STRATEGIC REPERTOIRE

With regular scenario practice the organisation builds its arsenal of future memories, filling in another piece of the futures puzzle (see figure 13.3, overleaf). Such an arsenal expands your anticipatory and interpretive reference points for unfolding novelty. At the same time, management expands its repertoire of strategies to respond to and exploit these futures. Having such a broad repertoire to call on is the key to better decision making in a turbulent and changing business environment.[10]

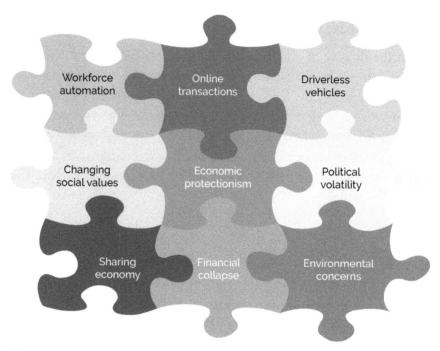

Figure 13.3: an arsenal of future memories

Each scenario exercise provides another piece of the futures puzzle, effectively building the organisation's arsenal of future memories and management's repertoire of strategic responses.

And what's the ultimate benefit of this institutionalised proficiency? You get a head start when you need it most—when the environment suddenly changes. To the unrehearsed mind, unexpected discontinuities reduce managerial competence to that of a novice, overwhelmed by the perceived speed and complexity of change.

To the prepared organisation, on the other hand, these discontinuities are greeted with a feeling of familiarity ('We've been here before and we know what to do'). Scenarios therefore enable management to skip the costly and resource-intensive stage of conscious incompetence ('What's happening?' and 'What do we do?'), and move directly to the more advanced, purposeful phase of conscious competence (see figure 13.4).

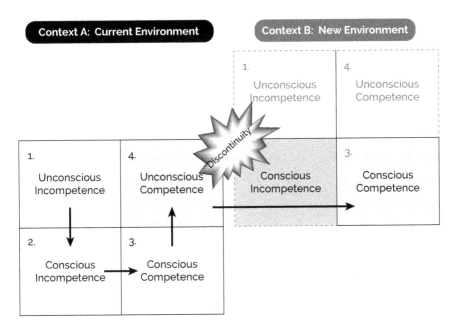

Figure 13.4: the scenario advantage

Scenarios enable management to move directly to the purposeful stage of conscious competence when discontinuities occur, providing a head start on their consciously incompetent competitors.

This advantage can last for years, or indeed it can be perpetual. While competitors attempt to muddle their way through the zone of conscious incompetence, the scenario-proficient organisation acts with the purpose that comes with familiarity and know-how. And with such proficiency, environmental turbulence is reframed from being a threat to being welcomed as the essential catalyst for ongoing growth. This is the strategic advantage delivered by scenarios.

ENDNOTES

Acknowledgements

1. Beck, D & Cowan, C (1996). *Spiral Dynamics: Mastering values, leadership, and change*, Blackwell, Oxford.
2. Inayatullah, S (2005). *Questioning the Future: Methods and tools for organizational and societal transformation*, 2nd edition, Tamkang University Press, Taipei.
3. Bawden, R (2000). *Learning from the Future: Of systems, scenarios and strategies* (PDF workbook).

Introduction

1. Wack, P (1984). *Scenarios: The gentle art of re-perceiving*, December 1984, Harvard Business School (unpublished manuscript).
2. van der Heijden, K (2005). *Scenarios: The art of strategic conversation*, 2nd edition, Wiley, Chichester, p. xxi.

Chapter 1

1. Wack, P (1993). *Scenario planning: Planning in turbulent times*, presentation at Global Business Network (video available at the Pierre Wack Memorial Library, Kennington, UK.
2. Wack, P (1985a). 'Scenarios: Uncharted waters ahead', *Harvard Business Review*, September–October, pp. 73–89, 73.
3. Ansoff, I (1975). 'Managing strategic surprise by response to weak signals', *California Management Review*, Winter, vol. XVIII, no. 2, pp. 21–33, p. 22.
4. Senge, P (1990). *The Fifth Discipline: The art and practice of the learning organization*, Doubleday, New York, p. 176.

Chapter 2

1. Toffler, A (1985). *The Adaptive Corporation*, McGraw-Hill, New York, pp. 18–19.
2. Wilson, I (2003). *The Subtle Art of Strategy: Organizational planning in uncertain times*, Praeger, Westport, CT, p. 79.
3. Ringland, G (1998). *Scenario planning: Managing for the future*, Wiley, Chichester, p. ix.
4. van der Heijden, K, Bradfield, R, Burt, G, Cairns, G & Wright, G (2002). *The Sixth Sense: Accelerating organisational learning with scenarios*, Wiley, Chichester, p. 125.
5. Kahn, H (1962). *Thinking about the Unthinkable*, Avon, New York.
6. Kahn, H & Pepper, T (1979). *The Japanese Challenge: The success and failure of economic success*, Crowell, New York, p. 112.
7. Kahn, H (1960). *On Thermonuclear War*, Princeton UP, Princeton, NJ.
8. Kahn (1962), p. 19.
9. Kleiner, A (1996), *The Age of Heretics: Heroes, outlaws, and the forerunners of corporate change*, Currency Doubleday, New York, p. 166.
10. Wack (1985a), p. 88.
11. Kleiner (1996), p. 173.
12. Schwartz, P (1991). *The Art of the Long View: Planning for the future in an uncertain world*, Doubleday, New York, p. 9.
13. van der Heijden et al. (2002), p. 133.
14. Wack (1985a).
15. Wack, P (1985b). 'Scenarios: Shooting the rapids', *Harvard Business Review*, November–December, pp. 139–50.
16. Beck, P (1984). 'Debate over alternate scenarios replaces forecasts at Shell U.K.', *Journal of Business Forecasting*, Spring.
17. Schwartz (1991).
18. van der Heijden (2005).
19. de Geus, A (1988). 'Planning as Learning', *Harvard Business Review*, 66(2), pp. 70–74.
20. Jaworski, J (1998). *Synchronicity: The inner path of leadership*, Berrett-Koehler, San Francisco.
21. Schoemaker, P & van der Heijden, K (1993). 'Strategic planning at Royal Dutch/Shell', *Journal of Strategic Change*, vol. 2, pp. 157–71.
22. Malaska, P (1985). 'Multiple scenario approach and strategic behaviour in European companies', *Strategic Management Journal*, vol. 6, pp. 339–55, 345.
23. Linneman, R & Klein, H (1979). 'The use of multiple scenarios by U.S. industrial companies', *Long Range Planning*, 12(1), pp. 83–90.

24. Linneman, R & Klein, H (1983). 'The use of multiple scenarios by U.S. industrial companies: A comparison study 1977–81', *Long Range Planning*, 16(6), pp. 94–101.
25. Bradfield, R (2004). 'Origins and evolution of scenario techniques in the context of business', University of Strathclyde, Graduate School of Business, Working Paper Series, paper no. 2004–10, pp. 9–10.
26. Wilkinson, A (2008). 'Approaches to scenario building', UKERC Conference presentation.
27. Linneman & Klein (1979), p. 85.
28. Kleiner (1996), p. 171.
29. Schwartz (1991), p. 37.
30. Mischel, W, Ebbesen, E & Raskoff Zeiss, A (1972). 'Cognitive and attentional mechanisms in delay of gratification', *Journal of Personality and Social Psychology*, 21(2), pp. 204–18.
31. Brand, S (1999). *The Clock of the Long Now: Time and responsibility*, Basic Books, New York, p. 29.
32. Boulding, E (1978). 'The dynamics of imaging futures', *World Future Society Bulletin*, 12(5), pp. 7.
33. Barker, J (1993). *Paradigms: The business of discovering the future*, HarperCollins, New York, p. 208.
34. Curry, A (2012). *The Future of Futures*, Association of Professional Futurists ebook, pp. 13–14.
35. Martelli, A (2001), 'Scenario building and scenario planning: State of the art and prospects of evolution', *Futures Research Quarterly*, Summer, 17(2), p. 63.

Chapter 3

1. Mintzberg, H (2000). *The Rise and Fall of Strategic Planning*, Pearson Education, Harlow, UK, p. 23.
2. 'Forward,' Richard Slaughter, ed., The Knowledge Base of Futures Studies. Volume One, Foundations, Hawthorn, Victoria Australia, DDM Media Group, 1996, page xix.
3. Wack (1985b), p. 150.
4. Wack, P (1993). *Pierre Wack — Speech and interviews*, GBN Scenario Planning Seminar, San Francisco, 18 April 2003. The Pierre Wack Memorial Library, Templeton College, Oxford University.
5. Wack (1985a), p. 77.
6. Wilson (2003), p. 79.
7. Schwartz (1991), p. 9.

Chapter 4

1. Hamel, G (1996).'Strategy as revolution', *Harvard Business Review,* July–August, pp. 69–82.
2. Ackoff, R (1977).'The corporate rain dance', *The Wharton Magazine,* pp. 36–41.
3. Kleiner, A (2013).'The dynamic capabilities of David Teece', *strategy+business,* November 2013.
4. Beck, PW (1983).'Forecasts: Opiates for decision makers', lecture to the Third International Symposium on Forecasting, Philadelphia, 5 June.
5. In relation to the limitations of traditional consumer research, Henry Ford is credited with the words,'If I had asked people what they wanted they would have said faster horses'.Whether or not Ford actually said this is contested.
6. Beck (1984), p. 4.
7. de Geus, A (1997). *The Living Company: Habits for survival in a turbulent business environment,* Harvard Business School Press, Boston, MA.
8. Michael, D (1973). *On Learning to Plan and Planning to Learn,* Jossey-Bass, San Francisco.
9. Choo, CW (2002). *Information Management for the Intelligent Organization: The art of scanning the environment,* 3rd edition, Information Today Inc., New Jersey, p. 247.
10. Beck (1983).
11. Beck (1984), p. 6.
12. Burt, G (2006).'Pre-determined elements in the business environment: Reflecting on the legacy of Pierre Wack', *Futures,* 38, pp. 830–40.
13. de Geus, A (2005).'Decision-taking and how to accelerate it', www.ariedegeus.com/talks.
14. Kiechel, W (1982).'Corporate strategists under fire', *Fortune,* 27 December, p. 38.
15. Charan, R & Colvin, G (1999).'Why CEOs fail', *Fortune,* 21 June.
16. Mintzberg, H (1994). *The Rise and Fall of Strategic Planning,* Prentice Hall, London, p. 26.
17. de Geus (2005).
18. de Geus (2005).
19. de Geus (2005).
20. de Geus (2005).
21. de Geus (1997), p. 58.
22. de Geus (2005).

Chapter 5

1. *The Roanoke Times,*'Some say it's "dumbest thing the city has ever done"', 20 September 2004, p. A1.
2. Suzuki, S (2006). *Zen Mind, Beginner's Mind,* p. 1.

3. Senge (1990), p. 176.
4. Stopford, M (2009). *Maritime Economics*, 3rd edition, Routledge, New York, p. 739.
5. Course notes, Oxford Scenarios Programme, Said Business School, Oxford, June 2007.
6. Levitt, T (2008). *Marketing Myopia*, Harvard Business School Publishing Corporation, Boston, MA, pp. 17–18.

Chapter 6

1. Molitor, G (2003). 'Molitor forecasting model: Key dimensions for plotting the "patterns of change"', *Journal of Futures Studies*, August, 8(1), pp. 61–72.
2. Curry, A & Hodgson, A (2008). 'Seeing in multiple horizons: Connecting futures to strategy', *Journal of Futures Studies*, August, 13(1), pp. 1–20.
3. Inayatullah (2000), p. 100.
4. Schwartz, P & Randall, D (2007). 'Ahead of the curve: Anticipating strategic surprises', from *Blindsides: How to anticipate forcing events and wild cards in global politics*, edited by Francis Fukuyama, American Interest Books, chapter 9.
5. Schultz, W (2010). 'Future tools: Scanning, futures wheels, Verge', August 30, www.slideshare.net.
6. 'Three Australian cricketers leave South Africa with bans for ball tampering', CNN, 29 March 2018.
7. 'Australia's Most Trusted Professions 2013', *Reader's Digest*, July 2013.
8. Kleiner, A (2003). 'The man who saw the future', *strategy+business*, Spring 2003, issue 30, 12 February.
9. Inayatullah, S (2010). World Futures Studies Federation Listserv correspondence, 10 July 2009.
10. Simon, H (1971). 'Designing organizations for an information-rich world', *Computers, Communication, and the Public Interest*, Johns Hopkins Press, Baltimore, MD, pp. 40–1.
11. 'Tobacco industry denies cancer tie', *New York Times*, 14 April 1954, p. 51.
12. Shand, A (2007). *Big Shots*, Penguin, Camberwell, UK, p. 36.
13. Inayatullah (2000), p. 44.
14. Sorokin, P (1957). *Social and Cultural Dynamics: A study of change in major systems of art, truth, ethics, law and social relationships*, Porter Sargent, Boston, MA, p. 681.
15. Graves, C (1974). 'Human nature prepares for a momentous leap', *The Futurist*, April, pp. 72–87.
16. Inglehart, R, Basañez, M & Moreno, A (1998). *Human Values and Beliefs: A cross-cultural sourcebook*, University of Michigan Press, p. 10.
17. Graves (1974), pp. 72–87.
18. Graves (1974), pp. 72–87.
19. Inglehart et al. (1998).

20. Maslow, A (1943). 'A theory of human motivation', *Psychological Review*, 50, pp. 370–96.
21. Inglehart, R (2000). 'Globalization and postmodern values', *The Washington Quarterly*, Winter, 23(1) pp. 215–28.
22. Inglehart (2000), p. 220.
23. Inglehart et al. (1998), p. 10.
24. Inglehart et al. (1998), p. 10.
25. Graves (1974), pp. 72–87.

Chapter 7

1. Mitroff, I (1988) *Break-Away Thinking: How to challenge your business assumptions and why you should*, Wiley, New York, p. 65.
2. Adapted from R Nelson (2007), Extending Foresight, presentation to 3rd Conference on Foresight, Strathclyde Business School, Glasgow, Scotland, 16–18 August.
3. Ogilvy, J & Schwartz, P (1998). 'Plotting your scenarios', from *Learning from the future: Competitive foresight scenarios*, edited by Liam Fahey and Robert Randall, Wiley, p. 59.

Chapter 8

1. de Bono, E (2006). *Edward de Bono's thinking course: Powerful tools to transform your thinking*, BBC Active, Harlow, p. 36.
2. Addy, J (2004) Suggested fifth stage of conscious competence model, www.businessballs.com/consciouscompetencelearningmodel.htm, accessed 12th August 2014.
3. Senge (1990), p. 190.
4. Barnett, S (1992). The Nissan Report, Bantam Doubleday Dell, New York, p. 135.
5. Barnett (1992), p. 138.
6. Senge (1990), p. 176.
7. van der Heijden (2005).
8. This question was posed by lecturer Dr Joseph Voros to our class of second-year strategic foresight students in 2006.
9. Amara, R & Lipinski, A (1983). *Business Planning for an Uncertain Future: Scenarios and strategies*, Pergamon Press, New York, pp. 49–51.
10. Amara & Lipinski (1983). p. 50.
11. Duncan, N & Wack, P (1994). 'Scenarios designed to improve decision-making', *Planning Review*, July/August 22(4), p. 23.
12. van der Heijden (2005), p. 177.
13. van der Heijden (2005), p. 176.
14. Amara & Lipinski (1983), p. 51.
15. van der Heijden (2005), p. 176.
16. Harman, W (1979). *An Incomplete Guide to the Future*, Norton, New York, p. 24.

Chapter 9

1. Wilber, K (1997).'An integral theory of consciousness', *Journal of Consciousness Studies*, 4(1), pp. 71–92.
2. Wotherspoon, S (2008).'Once were outcasts', *Herald Sun*, 15 March.
3. Voros, J (2006).'Integral environmental scanning', Foresight Methodologies 2, Strategic Foresight Master's Program course notes, Swinburne University of Technology.
4. Voros, J (ed.) (2003). *Reframing Environmental Scanning: A reader on the art of scanning the environment*, Australian Foresight Institute Monograph Series, no. 4, Swinburne University Press, Melbourne, p. 3.
5. 'Is our love affair with consumption over?', *Byron Shire Echo*, 25(51), 31 May 2011, p. 10.
6. 'Myer celebrates grand opening of renovated Bourke Street store', *Herald Sun*, 1 April 2011.
7. 'Making the sales pitch', *Sunday Herald Sun*, 25 March 2012.
8. 'Why online retailing is a dead-end: Gerry Harvey', *SmartCompany*, 26 November 2008.
9. Hamilton, C & Denniss, R (2005). *Affluenza: When too much is never enough*, Allen & Unwin, Crows Nest, Sydney.
10. Ray, P & Anderson, SR (2000). *The Cultural Creatives: How 50 million people are changing the world*, Three Rivers Press, New York.
11. Botsman, R (2010). TedX Sydney, May 22.

Chapter 10

1. Honton, E & Huss, W (1987).'Scenario planning—what style should you use?', *Long Range Planning*, 20(4), pp. 21–9.
2. Cairns, G & Wright, G (2011). *Scenario Thinking: Practical approaches to the future*, Palgrave Macmillan, Basingstoke, UK, p. 31.
3. Cairns & Wright (2011), pp. 30–1.
4. Cairns & Wright (2001), p. 31.
5. Ralston, B & Wilson, I (2006). *The Scenario Planning Handbook: Developing strategy for uncertain times*, Thomson/South-Western, pp. 104–5.
6. Ralston & Wilson (2006), p. 107.
7. Wilson, I (1998).'Mental maps of the future: An intuitive logics approach to scenarios', I Fahey, L & Randall, R (eds), *Learning from the Future: Competitive foresight scenarios*, Wiley, p. 89.
8. Schwartz, P (1991), p. 112.
9. Ralston & Wilson (2006), p. 115.
10. Worthington, B (2017).'Dairy crisis: Understanding why the bubble burst and what it means for milk in supermarkets', *ABC News*, 27 January 2017.

11. Flowers, B (2003). 'The art and strategy of scenario writing', *Strategy and Leadership*, 31(2), pp. 29–33.
12. Cascio, J (2010). 'Futures thinking: Scenario writing', *Fast Company*, February 2010.
13. Flowers (2003), p. 29.

Chapter 11

1. de Groot, AD (1965). *Thought and Choice in Chess*, Mouton, The Hague.
2. Perkins, D (1995). *Outsmarting IQ: The emerging science of learning intelligence*, The Free Press, New York, p. 81.
3. van der Heijden, K, Bradfield, R, Burt, G, Cairns, G & Wright, G (2002). *The Sixth Sense: Accelerating organisational learning with scenarios*, Wiley, Chichester, p. 75.
4. van der Heijden (2005), p. 129.
5. van der Heijden (2005), p. 129.
6. Ontario Ministry of Energy, Northern Development and Mines, www.mndm.gov.on.ca, July 2018.
7. *Victorian Public Libraries 2030: Strategic Framework*. This comprehensive strategic framework is available on the Public Libraries Victoria Network website, www.publiclibrariesvictoria.net.au/. *Victorian Public Libraries 2030* was a joint project led by the Victorian State Library and the Public Libraries Victoria Network. The author would like to acknowledge the State Library of Victoria and Public Libraries Victoria Network in allowing the reproduction of sections of the Framework.
8. van der Heijden (2005), p. xx.
9. Giesecke, J (1998). *Scenario Planning for Libraries*, American Library Association, Chicago, p. 22.

Chapter 12

1. Siegmann, K (2016). *Victorian Public Libraries 2030: The Future in Action*, ALIA, ACT.

Chapter 13

1. TV anchor Howard Beale (played by Peter Finch), in the 1976 film *Network*, written by Paddy Chayefsky.
2. Wohlstetter, R (1962.) *Pearl Harbor: Warning and decision*, Stanford University Press, Stanford, CA, p. 387.
3. Ingvar, D (1985). 'Memory of the future', *Human Neurobiology*, 4(3), pp. 127–36.
4. de Geus, A (1997), p. 36.
5. van der Heijden (2005), p. 138.

6. Kahn, J (2007) Wayne Gretzky-Style 'Field Sense' May Be Teachable, *Wired*, 22nd June 2007, http://www.wired.com/2007/05/ff-mindgames/" www.wired.com/2007/05/ff-mindgames/, accessed 12th May 2016.
7. Kahn, J (2007)
8. Schwartz, P (1991), p. 64.
9. Marcus, G (ed.) (1998). *Corporate Futures*, vol. v of the Late Editions Series, University of Chicago Press, Chicago.
10. Perkins, D (1995), p. 91.

INDEX

Lightning Source UK Ltd.
Milton Keynes UK
UKHW022059271119
354312UK00005B/21/P